MANAGING
TALENT

PHILIP SADLER

MANAGING TALENT

TALENT

MAKING THE BEST OF THE BEST

FINANCIAL TIMES

PITMAN PUBLISHING

PITMAN PUBLISHING
128 Long Acre, London WC2E 9AN

A division of Pearson Professional Limited

Originally published 1993 by Century Business
in association with The Economist Books Ltd

First published by Pitman Publishing 1993

A CIP catalogue record for this book can be obtained from the British Library.

ISBN 0 273 60533 X ✓

Printed and bound in Great Britain

Ashridge is a charity number 311906 registered as Ashridge (Bonar Law Memorial) Trust

CONTENTS

LIST OF FIGURES AND TABLES

Figures

Tables

ACKNOWLEDGEMENTS

Many people have contributed to this work. The greater part of the interviewing was carried out in a highly professional manner by Keith Milmer, Economic and Social Research Council fellow at Ashridge Management College, and Coralie Palmer. Keith also contributed many useful ideas and was largely responsible for Chapter 11. Preliminary telephone interviews were ably carried out by Dena Pearce and Kim Bennett has coped wonderfully well with successive drafts of the manuscript.

I am grateful for the encouragement of Sarah Child, formerly of The Economist Books, and for the moral and financial support of Ashridge Management College, which made it possible to conduct a number of interviews in the USA. At Ashridge, Michael Osbaldeston, chief executive, gave the project his personal backing and Valerie Hammond, director of the Ashridge Management Research Group, kindly made a room available in her department. Margaret Dawson of the same group provided invaluable administrative assistance. In the early stages Virginia Merritt's enthusiasm got the project off the ground. I have also benefited from the untiring efforts of the Ashridge library staff and from Richard Bamsey's skill with artwork.

I also acknowledge the contribution of the London Human Resource Group.

My thanks are due to all those in companies who gave of their time to be interviewed. Those willing to be mentioned by name are listed in the Appendix.

I am very appreciative of the support and tolerance of my wife Terry who has carried more than her share of domestic burdens while the book was in preparation.

Finally I would like to acknowledge my great debt to Peter Drucker whose ideas on the subject, first expressed in 1969, stimulated my own interest in it.

Acknowledgements are also due to Penguin Books for permission to publish the cartoons on pages 51 and 79 from the Collection of Alex Strips.

Philip Sadler
August 1992

INTRODUCTION

The central theme of this book brings together two sets of ideas which have been gathering support and gaining in relevance over the last 25 years.

The first is that, in the modern world, the prosperity of nations and the competitiveness of corporations depends chiefly upon the extent to which human talent is developed and applied to the wealth creation process.

The second is more controversial. It is that the traditional forms of organisation of work and processes of management are becoming increasingly inappropriate as the proportion of "knowledge workers", or highly qualified, talented people in the workforce grows.

I first became aware of this second issue when engaged in human factors research with the UK's Royal Air Force. In 1960 I presented a paper to the NATO symposium on Defence Psychology[1] with the title "Technical Change and Military Social Structure". The theme of the paper was that the traditional forms of military organisation and command functions were becoming more and more inappropriate as military technology became more complex and required growing numbers of technically qualified personnel to operate and maintain it. Although the term "knowledge workers" was not yet in use, the issues addressed – questions of organisation, career structures, motivation and management style – were the same as those which have been highlighted more recently in industry and commerce. It is interesting to note that for a time the Royal Air Force responded to the need for technical specialists to have career opportunities other than through the command structure by introducing a "technician ladder". (This experiment was later abandoned on the grounds that it caused confusion and blurred the clarity of the chain of command.)

Both issues came into sharper focus for me on reading Peter Drucker's *Age of Discontinuity*[2] in 1969, by which time I was involved in teaching and research in the industrial management field. The central theme of his work was the emergence of "knowledge-intensive"

1

industry as the principal agent of wealth creation, taking the place of the traditional capital- and labour-intensive industries of the industrial revolution. He pointed to two key differences between the newer industries such as electronics, software engineering and pharmaceuticals and the older ones such as steel, shipbuilding and automobile manufacturing.

- The newer industries' most important resource and source of competitive advantage was neither capital nor labour but knowledge, and knowledge, moreover, that was in need of constant renewal.
- The employees of the new industries were, relative to the traditional ones, more highly educated, more highly qualified and with different needs, expectations and patterns of motivation. They were neither blue-collar workers nor white-collar workers of the traditional kind, like bank clerks or shop assistants. They were "knowledge workers", or as they have more recently been called, "gold-collar workers".

Once Drucker's analysis had opened my eyes the idea that in the modern world knowledge, rather than capital or labour, was the most precious commodity seemed to me to be self-evident. Yet as time went by I realised that this insight was not shared by the majority of those in government and industry responsible for shaping policy, whether at the macroeconomic level or at the level of the enterprise. In the UK, in particular, the persistent failure on the part of successive governments to invest adequately in education, training and research, coupled with the negative or apathetic attitude of many large businesses to these vital forms of investment, led to the conclusion that most decision-makers were still operating with outmoded models of economic life.

Also in 1969, having up to that point in my career been a research sociologist and thus one of the new breed of "knowledge workers" myself, overnight and without preparation I became chief executive of a knowledge-intensive organisation – Ashridge Management College – a position I was to hold for the next 20 years.

In this role I had to learn on the one hand how to manage knowledge workers so as to meet their needs for challenging work assignments, autonomy and "space", and on the other to ensure the economic viability of a college entirely without subsidy from public or private funding sources. I found almost all the literature on management and organisation singularly unhelpful in this process, based as it was on assumptions about the nature of management and the effectiveness of organisation structures which, however valid in conventional industrial settings, did not apply in this case. I gained a number of insights from this experience.

- I found out very quickly that highly educated and talented people have to be managed in ways which are rather different from the standard and traditional ones in the management textbooks. In particular they required, if they were to be fully productive, more freedom, more autonomy, more communication and to be treated more as individuals. Trying to arrive at meaningful and equitable assessments of performance was particularly difficult.

- As the number of staff grew it seemed the natural thing to do to invite some of them to assume management responsibilities, so I quickly discovered that the qualities and skills involved in being an outstanding lecturer or researcher were quite different from those involved in successful management. Turning specialists into effective managers remained a constant problem. From this arose the need to provide career progression other than in consequence of assuming a managerial role.

- I learned that it was not so much knowledge that led to wealth creation as the broader attribute of talent. The most successful among the staff were by no means those possessing the deepest levels of knowledge. They were the ones with much more elusive qualities; those able to inspire, to stimulate and to provide leadership in the classroom. Trying to define these elusive qualities and select for them proved an extremely challenging task.

On retiring from my post at Ashridge and with the opportunity to return to research I formed the idea of writing this book with the hope that it might prove helpful to others with the responsibility for managing highly talented people. The ideas in it have three sources.

- Although I have not made explicit reference to Ashridge, the experience has undoubtedly influenced my whole approach to the subject and, hopefully, has ensured that I avoid flights of academic fancy.

- I have studied the literature which is relevant to my subject matter and I have referred to it whenever I have found it to be helpful.

- I have drawn on the experiences and practices of some 50 com-

3

panies in the UK, continental Europe and the USA. It would be claiming too much to say that rigorous structured interviews were conducted in these companies. Rather it is better to say that conversations took place with key people in them, either chief executives or senior people in the human resources field. The aim was not to seek statistically valid data but to elicit a range of ideas, insights, attitudes and descriptions of practice so as to provide a rich source of material drawn from contemporary industrial situations. The companies involved were not selected according to any rigorous sampling criteria. The aim was to obtain information from organisations varying in size and in the extent to which they could be described as "knowledge-intensive" or "talent-intensive". It was felt important, too, that they should be drawn from different national cultures. The companies which kindly agreed to co-operate with the research are listed in the Appendix together with the names of the respondents. (In only two cases, both in the UK, did companies request that their participation should remain anonymous.)

As the final element in this introduction I should like to answer the inevitable criticism that this book is "elitist" in that it focuses exclusively on what remains a small fraction of the total working population of even the most advanced countries and ignores the abilities and contribution to wealth creation of the large majority of workers. It is a criticism to which I am sensitive, since I do place a high value on human beings regardless of whether or not they possess outstanding talent. It nevertheless remains inescapably true that abilities are unevenly distributed among the population and that organisations of many different kinds depend disproportionately on the talented minority for their success. No one would argue against the idea that it is the leading dancers that chiefly determine the fortunes of a ballet company rather than the scene-shifters, and that in consequence it is rather more important to manage the leading dancers effectively than the scene-shifters. At the same time it remains true that a strike by the scene-shifters can halt performances and cause a financial crisis. It is also the case, in my view, that in the long run the successful company will be the one in which the leading dancers, the chorus, the administrative staff and the scene-shifters along with the commercial and artistic directors all feel part of the same team.

It is certainly the case that although the core talent at Ashridge Management College was the high calibre teaching staff, the college's very considerable success was due to the way in which these able people were supported by others whose talents lay in different fields, and in areas which society chooses not to reward so highly. Ashridge owes much to its highly talented personnel in these other fields. Their competence resulted in world class standards of hotel services, and a degree of dedicated administrative support to the "front line" which is rarely encountered. This book, therefore, is respectfully dedicated to the talented catering staff, gardeners, secretaries, maintenance workers, drivers, receptionists, librarians, computer technicians, media specialists and others whose skill and dedication was so vital, not forgetting Bill and Sid, the two stonemasons whose own outstanding talents would, in another age, have commanded greater recognition.

References
1 Philip Sadler, "Technical Change and Military Social Structure" in F. Geldard (ed.), *Defence Psychology*, London, Pergamon Press, 1962.
2 Peter Drucker, *The Age of Discontinuity*, London, Heinemann, 1969.

1

THE TALENT-INTENSIVE ORGANISATION

The economic transformation taking place in the world's most developed economies during the second half of the twentieth century has been described by Alvin Toffler[1] as "the third wave". He saw it as having the same significance for the development of human society as the two previous revolutions: the agrarian and the industrial. There is no doubt that the changes in the nature of economic activity are fundamental. They include the growth of services as a source of both employment and output and the increasing importance of knowledge as a factor of production in the so-called post-industrial or information society.

Knowledge as a factor of production

The growing importance of the ownership and control of knowledge and information as sources of power in society, and the related emergence of the "knowledge-intensive" organisation alongside the "capital-intensive" and "labour-intensive" organisations of the past, had been discussed some years earlier by Daniel Bell.[2] Whereas the traditional "commanding heights" of the industrial society were either labour-intensive, such as coal mining or textiles, or capital-intensive, such as steel making, or a mixture of the two such as automobile manufacturing, he pointed out that in the industries of growing economic significance, such as pharmaceuticals, computer software, professional services and financial services, the major assets are the people.

What is meant by knowledge in this context? Partly it means scientific knowledge in terms of the natural sciences – physics, mathematics, chemistry and biology – and partly it means knowledge about the applications of science (technological know-how) in such fields as medicine and engineering. It also includes, however, knowledge from the fields of social science, psychology and law as well as the kind of knowledge used in an advertising agency or by a management consultant, an expert in fine art or the investment manager of a pension fund.

Ernest Woodruffe, in his address to the annual general meeting of

Unilever in London as long ago as 1972, made what may well be the first public acknowledgement by the chairman of a major company that knowledge was its key resource. Unilever, he said, had competitors who had similar access to capital, who were often less heavily taxed, and sometimes treated benevolently in other ways by their governments. What they lacked, however, was the "immense body of varied knowledge and commercial skills which Unilever has built up over the years".

He went on to indicate the wide range of knowledge involved: knowing when, where and for how long to borrow money; the combination of technological, mathematical and computer skills involved in changing the composition of margarine without loss of quality when the relative prices of oils and fats change; the understanding which tells the company whether and when to distribute free samples to peoples' homes in order to increase market share; or knowledge of housewives' tastes.

> "In every aspect of the business knowledge is vital; and much of the knowledge which is important to a firm like Unilever cannot be found in books; it has to be acquired often expensively, sometimes painfully, by experience and deliberate enquiry.
>
> Knowledge is not cheap. Around the world we spend many millions in acquiring it. But without this expenditure we could not survive against competition.
>
> The economies of using knowledge over and over again, everywhere adapting it to local needs, are very great. Knowledge has no marginal cost. It costs no more to use it in the 70 countries in which we operate than in one. It is the principle which makes Unilever economically viable. The knowledge Unilever has is both extensive and complex. It is the source of your profits and of the main benefits Unilever brings to the peoples of the countries in which it operates."

The distinguishing features
Knowledge has a number of distinguishing features when compared with the other factors involved in wealth creation: land, labour and capital.

1 It cannot be consumed. If one person or institution uses some land or some labour or some capital it is not possible for some other person or institution simultaneously to make use of the same resource. Yet with knowledge this is possible. Any number of persons can use

the same piece of knowledge at the same time without in any way depleting it.

Although knowledge cannot be used up or destroyed in this way, it can be allowed to become obsolete through failure to maintain it by bringing it up to date. It can also be lost if allowed to remain in the memory store of the human brain instead of being transferred to paper or computer memory.

2 Knowledge as property is much harder to protect compared with property in the form of land or capital, or indeed the slave labour of the past. Much of the knowledge that a firm possesses cannot be patented and moves to competing organisations as employees move from one firm to another. It may not be lost to the first firm if it has been carefully recorded, but its value as a source of competitive advantage will have been greatly diminished.

3 It is extremely difficult to quantify the impact of knowledge on the wealth creation process. This is true both at the macroeconomic level and at the level of the enterprise. Economists have the ability to measure the crop yield from a given area of land, they can measure the return on investment of capital and they can measure the pro- ductivity of labour. They are not capable, however, of measuring with any precision how efficiently knowledge is being used, despite the fact that it is the major investment expenditure of the modern economy as well as its key resource. Similarly, industrialists can normally say how much capital there is in the business and how much labour is employed, but ask them to say how much knowledge and of what kinds exists in the business and only the most vague and imprecise answers will result. Stonier[3] argues that the greatest challenge facing economists in the modern world is to find better ways of answering such questions.

The extent to which an industry or an individual enterprise is knowledge-intensive can be approximately assessed, however, by tak- ing as an indicator the percentage of qualified manpower employed. Using such an indicator it can be seen that the shift from capital- and labour-intensive production to knowledge-intensive production is every bit as important in the process of transition to a post-industrial or post-business economy as the shift from manufacturing to services.

Knowledge adds value

In the 1980s there was a boom in US manufactured goods exports. In just six years from 1986 to 1991 these almost doubled. The boom was not only unprecedented in US history but was unique in the history of the world economy. At first sight there might not appear to be any pattern in the range of goods involved in this rapid upsurge; they included jet engines, heart valves, sophisticated software, movies and body scanners. The firms involved included giants such as GE and Boeing, a large number of medium-sized firms and many tiny companies. The common factor, however, as Peter Drucker[4] points out, is clear product differentiation. These are not commodities. Although they may be priced competitively they are not sold on price. The success lies in the area of high added-value goods; and what adds value is knowledge. This ranges from the scientific and engineering knowledge built into body scanners and aircraft engines to the kind of ingenuity which resulted in the 3M "Post-its". In Drucker's view, this surge in high price manufactures was the most significant economic event of the decade.

There are two kinds of foreign direct investment. On the one hand there is the kind exemplified by early investment in the UK by Ford and General Motors or more recent investment by Nissan which transfers knowledge (in these cases, vastly superior production technology) along with capital. On the other there is the kind which involves capital transfers but adds little or no new knowledge as in the case of most UK investment in the USA in the 1980s. The former kind is immeasurably more beneficial to the host country than the latter, yet how many government agencies seeking to encourage inward investment take account of the difference, or are even aware of it?

Knowledge-intensive industries

The means by which much knowledge is harnessed to the wealth creation process is information technology, just as the means by which capital is harnessed is production technology. Increasingly those functions of the human being which are involved in processing information – computing, memory, information retrieval, and so on – can now be carried out at ever-increasing speed with ever-decreasing cost by a range of electronic and optical devices. Knowledge-intensive industries are also information-intensive; their future, including their requirements for human resources and their forms of organisation, will to a large extent reflect further developments in IT including expert systems and artificial intelligence.

Knowledge industries such as business, professional and financial services are classified as tertiary industries to distinguish them from primary industries (agriculture, forestry, fishing and mining) and secondary industries (manufacturing, construction and the utilities). However, Drucker[5] argues, knowledge industry generally has become the modern world's primary industry since it supplies to the economy the essential and central production resource. Once the farmer was the backbone of the economy. Then it was the factory worker, exemplified by the view that what was good for General Motors was good for the USA. Today it is the knowledge professional.

The demand for knowledge workers in the future seems insatiable. It is not just the university chemists, physicists and engineers who get attractive consulting assignments, often to the point that they have a larger income from consulting outside the university than from teaching and research inside. Geographers, mathematicians, economists, linguists, business school faculty and psychologists are all in demand. Few areas of learning are not being tapped by the business organisations of modern society.

Broadening the knowledge concept: the talent-intensive organisation

The term "knowledge industry" appears to have been coined by the Princeton economist, Fritz Machlup, in his book *The Production and Distribution of Knowledge in the US*.[6] Knowledge, even if broadly defined so as to include pure science at one end of the scale and marketing know-how at the other, is undoubtedly of key importance. Sooner or later, however, all knowledge is freely available. The true source of competitive advantage is not so much knowledge as talent, which is the only remaining scarce resource.

The structure of the post-industrial enterprise, therefore, is better described as talent-intensive rather than knowledge-intensive. Talent has more to do with abilities, aptitudes, skills and personal qualities than with knowledge. In some occupations, knowledge outweighs aptitude, skill or personal qualities, as in the case of the theoretical physicist; in other cases, such as the professional tennis player, skill is the most important factor. In some instances knowledge and skill are finely balanced; examples include the court room lawyer combining legal knowledge with skill as an advocate, or the brain surgeon combining knowledge of the human nervous system with delicate surgical skills. Some highly talented people possess no academic or professional qualifications whatsoever, yet their economic value, based on skill, is extraordinary. Many film stars, pop stars and sports players fall into this category. In other instances it is neither knowledge nor skill but personal attributes, such as the elusive element known as "star" quality in the world of entertainment, which define talent. Expertise is a term which brings knowledge and talent together. According to a report by the London Human Resource Group,[7] institutions in the City of London do not buy and sell money in the classical sense nowadays. They buy and sell expertise.

Many kinds of talented people typically work alone. The nature of their work is such that they would not easily fit into an organisational framework. Obvious examples include artists, composers and writers. If such people are to exploit their talent commercially, however, they have to do so through organisations, often quite large ones, like publishers, dealers and agencies. One of the companies co-operating in the research is EMI Music, one of the world's largest producers of recorded popular music. EMI does not employ the artists who feature on its record labels but in a very important sense it manages their creative output; it has no choice, since its own survival depends upon its ability to find, develop, nurture and retain a competitive share of the most successful individuals and groups on the pop music scene.

There is a second category of talented people who face some clear choices; they can choose to be self-employed, to enter into partnership or to join a large firm. Such choices typically face lawyers, accountants, designers and architects. The commercial value of their work is reflected by the rapid growth in recent years of large, global enterprises employing professionals in such fields as accountancy and business services. Firms like KPMG Peat Marwick, Price Waterhouse and Andersen Consulting employ thousands of qualified persons in many countries.

Finally there are talented people who would have difficulty in finding an outlet for their talents other than in the context of a large organisation. This may be because of the cost of the facilities to which they need access. The nuclear physicist cannot build a particle accelerator in a garden shed. There are also those whose talents are such that they are best suited to managerial work; who are, by definition, organisation people.

Organisations, typically, are designed to minimise rather than encourage individuality. Emphasis is placed on uniformity, standardisation, control, predictability, stability and order. Standard operating procedures are preferred over virtuoso performances and routine is more acceptable than drama. Small wonder, therefore, that when we try to constrain the activities of highly individualistic, talented people within the framework of the traditional organisation, problems and difficulties arise. In the modern world, however, the problem cannot be avoided. Huge industries have grown up in fields in which the only truly productive resource is human talent of one kind or another.

The talent-intensive society

The society based on an economy which is characterised by talent-intensive industry has some salient features.

1 The social framework. This is changing from one of predetermined occupations into one of choices for the individual. There are more opportunities for productive, rewarding and well-paid work than there are talented men and women available to fill them. Conversely, there are fewer opportunities for those at the other end of the scale.

Fifty years ago the work opportunities for educated and gifted people were few in number: the professions (law, medicine), the church, teaching, the civil service and, in industry, as engineers, accountants or chemists. Today the range encompasses archaeologists, biochemists and biologists, linguists, psychologists, statisticians, systems analysts, professional sports players, musicians, entertainers, directors, producers, specialists in public relations, advertisers and designers, to name a few.

2 Personnel. Modern society needs a substantial but balanced supply of scientific and technical people and people educated or trained in the humanist, political, economic, behavioural and artistic disciplines.

Above all, it needs people capable of understanding technology even though they themselves are not scientists or engineers and it needs people capable of understanding the arts, the social sciences, economics and political science even though they themselves have studied science or technology. It needs managers, namely people who can put knowledge to work, and leaders with the vision to point the way forward.

3 Knowledge and talent. Drucker makes a distinction between the intellectual view of knowledge and his concept of knowledge as a central resource in the economy. For the intellectual, knowledge can be found in a book. But for Drucker, knowledge, like electricity, is a form of energy that exists only when it is being used. The same applies to talent. It follows that economic success will accrue increasingly to those societies most competent in identifying, educating, developing and putting to work the talents of their populations. Competitive advantage will similarly accrue to those companies which attract, nurture and put to effective use the most talented of those moving from education to work.

Although these talented employees are not labourers or operatives, they are, nevertheless, employees. It is not necessarily productive, however, to tell them what to do or how to do it. On the contrary they are paid to apply their knowledge, ability or skill, which involves exercising judgment, taking decisions, acting responsibly.

Drucker argues that the hidden conflict between knowledge workers' view of themselves as having professional status and the employer's viewpoint which often sees (and treats) them as the upgraded and well-paid (even over-paid) successors of yesterday's skilled workers lies behind the disenchantment of so many highly educated young people with the jobs available to them. It explains why they protest so loudly against the "stupidity" of business. They expect to be treated as special and find themselves referred to collectively as "staff".

good call.

4 Work is not disappearing. While blue-collar workers may have more leisure, highly qualified workers in key positions are working longer hours, taking work home.

This book is about the managerial and organisational problems which commonly arise in talent-intensive organisations and about the processes which can be used to build sustainable bridges between the working environments which talented people need if they are to flourish, and the conditions which must exist if organisations are to survive and achieve their objectives in an increasingly competitive world. In particular it is written for those who have the power to take decisions about matters of management and organisation in enterprises in which a significant proportion of the workforce, in effect the "shop floor", is made up of talented personnel, sometimes referred to as "gold-collar workers". In such organisations the equivalents of the brain surgeon, the nuclear physicist or the university lecturer in medieval history are operatives. In some instances the number of highly talented employees is greater than the remainder of the personnel. The Institute of Manpower Studies in the UK is a typical example; its staff includes seven with PhDs, 15 with master's degrees and ten with first degrees.

The remaining staff, mainly clerical and secretarial workers, number 18. Somewhat larger in scale is a company contributing to this research – Glaxo Group Research Ltd – which employs 3,000 people of which 2,000 are graduates, including 600 with PhDs.

Characteristics of talent-intensive organisations

Talent-intensive organisations have six features in common.

1 People really are the organisation's principal assets. Countless organisations each year, in their annual reports, pay lip service to this notion. In the case of the talent-intensive organisation it really is so. These organisations are able to recover from serious financial losses, or from such disasters as the destruction of premises by fire, but the loss of a significant number of personnel can cause irreparable damage. Tom Lloyd,[8] for example, tells how the market capitalisation of the UK Investment Bank Hill Samuel fell by £44m following the departure of two star corporate finance executives. But the point is stronger than this. In an important sense the talented people represent the essential function of the organisation, its reason for existence. Without its brilliant faculty the Harvard Business School would be just another piece of real estate. Of what use would the plant, buildings and equipment of Rolls-Royce or Pratt & Whitney be without their aircraft engine design teams? In the labour-intensive organisation a high level of labour turnover is an irritant and can constitute an important element in costs but it is unlikely to be strategically significant; in the talent-intensive organisation it can drain its lifeblood.

2 Because the key assets of the talent-intensive organisation are people, they do not appear on the organisation's balance sheet. (Sports clubs which pay transfer fees are an interesting exception to this general rule and the implications of this will be returned to later.) The rules, conventions and traditions of the accountancy profession simply cannot cope with the task of accurately evaluating either the work or, indeed, the financial performance of talent-intensive organisations, the "return on human capital". There have been a number of attempts to develop and introduce some form of human asset accounting, but so far without success. This issue will be explored in Chapter 11.

3 The great source of vulnerability of the talent-intensive organisation is that its key assets are mobile; they can simply walk away, either to join the competition or to set up their own organisations.

4 The work that is the core activity of the talent-intensive organisation cannot be automated. Designers, brain surgeons, leaders and creative research scientists can take comfort from the fact that they will not be replaced by robots or computers. What will increasingly happen, however, is that their talents will be made very much more productive as a result of being allied to technology. Such developments as computer-aided design, computer-aided diagnosis, more and more powerful scientific instruments and the use of lasers in surgery are a few examples of an important trend.

5 There is an above-average reliance on creativity and innovation. Talented people are pathfinders rather than path followers. They give of their best in environments which nourish creativity and innovation.

6 In talent-intensive organisations there is a common tendency to perceive the key success criteria as other than financial. The culture is all about winning or accomplishing specific tasks or gaining recognition. For many architects, to win a major competition is of much greater importance than whether or not the contract that ensues will be profitable; the actor turns to the critical notices before asking about the box office takings; every sports club manager dreams about winning the cup, not about being the most profitable club in the league; the research scientist's ambition is to make that sensational breakthrough in knowledge; and the surgeon focuses on saving the patient's life. This makes the managerial task more difficult and more complex than in other kinds of organisation.

The international dimension

Human resources strategies must increasingly be framed in the context of the rapidly growing internationalisation of the "labour" market for talent. Other than in times of severe economic recession, such people as aircraft engine designers, microbiologists, software creators, tennis stars, pop singers or architects are in demand in excess of supply everywhere in the world. Traditional national standards in terms of salaries and benefits are increasingly irrelevant. Failure to face this fact, both nationally and at the level of the enterprise, has resulted in a steady flow of talent from countries with low living standards or high levels of personal taxation to richer countries or ones with less punitive taxes, the so-called "brain drain".

Peter Drucker has observed that this first happened after the American War of Independence, when American consuls bribed British textile engineers to migrate to America and teach their transatlantic cousins the technology of textile machinery. The process is basically the same as more recent cases involving microbiologists and other rare specialists.

An important element, therefore, in human resource strategy for the talent-intensive company, however small, is that the strategy must enable the business to get the talent it needs in the face of global competition. The alternative is to be slowly starved out of the market. It is also important that the strategy should be broad-based and not narrowly conceived in terms of compensation plans. Although salaries, stock options, "top hat" pensions, company cars and the like are obviously very important, it is clear from abundant evidence that other factors frequently carry greater weight with highly talented people. One of these is the reputation of the organisation in its field; is it at the leading edge, does it set the pace for its industry, is it simply a great company to work for?

In spite of relatively miserly salaries top US academics can be persuaded to spend at least part of their careers working at Oxford or Cambridge universities, while it would take a very big salary and benefits package to lure an outstanding British academic to an unknown US university in a remote southern state. Few people working with the British Broadcasting Corporation contemplate working anywhere else, while the same is true of IBM. Reputations of this kind, of course, take decades or even centuries to build. The challenge for new companies in newer industries is to work strategically for such eminence in their fields while adopting some other approaches in the interim.

Managing talented personnel

The material for this book is drawn from the experiences and approaches adopted by over 50 talent-intensive companies in the UK, continental Europe and the USA, and from a considerable body of research evidence which has been accumulated over the past decade or so. The issues which will be dealt with include recruiting and selection, induction, retention, career development, remuneration, motivation, performance management, organisation and management style.

The first requirement, however, is for the chief executive of the talent-intensive organisation to recognise its nature, to grasp the strategic significance of the fact that without an adequate supply of highly motivated, exceptional talent the organisation has no future, regardless of its current share price or level of financial reserves.

This recognition leads on to the fact that the organisation's human resource strategies are not merely appendages to the business plan but are in fact central components of overall business strategy.

SUMMARY

Bell, Toffler and others have drawn attention to the emergence of a new economic order: the post-industrial society, sometimes referred to as the post-business or information society. Two salient characteristics of the new order are a shift from manufacturing to services and from labour- and capital-intensive industries on the one hand to knowledge-intensive industries on the other. Knowledge in this context includes not only the natural sciences but the social sciences, psychology, law and "know-how" of the kind involved in management and marketing.

Knowledge as a factor of production has some important characteristics which affect the way it is managed. It cannot be consumed, but it is difficult to protect. It is extremely difficult to account for. Sooner or later, all knowledge is freely available. True competitive advantage rests not so much upon knowledge as upon talent. The structure of the post-industrial enterprise is better described as talent-intensive rather than knowledge-intensive.

Talent reflects ability, aptitude, skill or personal qualities. Although many talented people work alone, most are to be found in organisations. Organisations have not traditionally been designed to cope with highly talented individuals. The traditional hierarchical model of bureaucratic controls was developed in the context of labour-intensive industries. Not surprisingly, problems and difficulties arise in an economy characterised by talent-intensive industry. Such an economy offers an increasingly wide range of occupational choice for talented people. Economic success depends on making the best possible use of such talent, both at national levels and at the level of the enterprise, particularly the larger enterprises which employ thousands of talented people.

Talent-intensive organisations have several distinguishing features. People really are the most valuable assets, yet they do not appear on the balance sheet. These assets are mobile; they can simply walk away. The core activities resist automation consisting as they do of the highest levels of human ability expressed in work. Such organisations rely particularly on human creativity, and success is often defined in other than economic terms. The market for talent is international, so human-resource strategies must increasingly be framed in an international context.

The most important foundation for an appropriate and effective human-resource strategy, however, is the recognition, by top management, of the nature of the talent-intensive organisation with all the implications this carries. In these organisations human-resource strategy is a vital component of business strategy, not an appendage to it.

References

1 Alvin Toffler, *The Third Wave*, New York, William Morrow, 1980.
2 Daniel Bell, *The Coming of Post-Industrial Society*, New York, Basic Books, 1973.
3 Tom Stonier, *The Wealth of Information*, London, Methuen, 1983.
4 Peter Drucker, *Managing for the Future*, Oxford, Butterworth Heinemann, 1992.
5 Peter Drucker, *The Age of Discontinuity*, London, Heinemann, 1969.
6 Fritz Machlup, *The Production and Distribution of Knowledge in the US*, Princeton University Press, 1962.
7 Amin Rajan, *Capital People*, London, The Industrial Society, 1989.
8 Tom Lloyd, *The Nice Company*, London, Bloomsbury, 1990.

2

THE PSYCHOLOGISTS' VIEW
OF TALENT

By definition, highly talented people are extraordinary. Their special gifts, abilities or skills place them apart from the great majority of human beings. As a consequence their sense of uniqueness, of their own individuality, is almost certainly heightened compared with the average person.

This sense of being different, of being special, of unusual personal worth, is often built up from early childhood by the actions and reactions of others. Most parents are delighted by the discovery that a child is particularly talented in some field or other and the steady flow of warm parental approval engenders a strong sense of being special within the family. Most teachers show the same reaction to the discovery of a particularly talented pupil. The child develops an awareness of being special within the community. Where outstanding academic performance leads to a place at one of the great universities there follow the simultaneous discoveries that there are, indeed, other similarly talented people around, but that in relation to society as a whole they form a tiny elite.

At each of these formative stages the talented individual encounters admiration, envy, respect – all calculated to bolster self-esteem. This may become excessive; the individual may see rules as made for ordinary people and to be disregarded, while everyone else joins the conspiracy, excusing and forgiving. In later life this can lead to extremely eccentric, even outrageous behaviour. A recent biography revealed the artist, Eric Gill, as a sexual monster, committing numerous criminal acts of incest and bestiality yet accepted and protected by those closest to him who stood in awe of his talent.

Talented individuals are not, of course, entirely screened from negative feedback and for some, indeed, it is the negative aspects of being different which dominate their lives. Talented individuals soon learn that great things are expected of them; they come to set themselves very high standards; in consequence the sense of failure when expectations are not met can be devastating. Imagine being good enough at athletics to be selected to represent your country, only to finish well down the field in the first heat.

In circumstances in which talent is neither appreciated nor fostered, problems are still greater. There is a world of difference between the talented child of talented parentage – for example, a gifted musician born into a family already characterised by musical talent – and a "one-off", such as the child with an unusual aptitude for higher mathematics born into a working class family with no academic or intellectual tradition. In the latter case the experience may well be of the "ugly duckling" variety. The common factor, however, is the heightened sense of individuality which the possession of talent inevitably brings with it.

In many cases talent may never be recognised, leading to frustration, boredom, even to criminal behaviour. This can be the cause of many "people problems" in organisations, like absenteeism, turnover and conflict in industrial relations. More seriously it can lead to acts of sabotage, particularly in relation to computer software, and fraud of various kinds.

Talent is of course relative and our language recognises this. At the peak is genius – an overused term. Thereafter we use such words as brilliant, clever, gifted, talented, bright and the like to make a distinction between those who stand out and those who are merely competent or capable. Talented people are often well able to recognise and acknowledge superior talent. In the words of Arthur Conan Doyle: "Mediocrity knows nothing higher than itself, but talent instantly recognises genius."

Can talent be measured?

The most highly regarded early scientific work on talent was carried out by Francis Galton[1] who was himself in the genius class. He learned to read at the age of two and a half and wrote a letter before he was four; by the age of five he could read almost any English book and some French and could add, multiply and tell the time. This implies an intelligence quotient in the region of 200, a level not achieved by more than one child in 50,000. Galton maintained that mental capacities are hereditary. He proposed that mental ability followed a normal distribution with 14 classes of ability, each at equal intervals from its neighbours, with classes A–G above average and classes a–g below. A 15th and 16th class he labelled Genius and Idiocy. Galton's "natural ability" was, however, not a simple intelligence factor but a composite of intelligence, motivation and power. He argued that "eminence" is an adequate index to natural ability, since the truly able individual cannot be repressed by purely social obstacles such as the class system.

When children or adults are described as talented, gifted or bright the most usual implication is that they possess a very high level of general mental ability or intelligence. Over the years a huge amount of research effort has been expended in trying to define and measure intelligence and relate it to academic attainment, achievement in life and other variables. The first tests of intelligence were devised by Binet, a French psychologist, at the beginning of the 1920s. Over the years such tests have been refined and developed and brought into widespread use, both in education and in selection for employment. In recent years, however, they have increasingly become the targets of criticism.

The measurement of intelligence

The intelligence quotient (IQ) of a child is the ratio of his or her mental age, as indicated by intelligence test scores, and his or her chronological age. The average child would have the same mental age as chronological age and would therefore have an IQ of 100.

Mental capacity continues developing up to the age of 14 or 15 although in exceptional cases of late developers it may continue beyond this up to 18 or even 20 years of age. For the purpose of calculating IQ, however, an age of more than 15 is reckoned as 15.

The tests are so constructed that IQs follow a normal, bell-shaped, distribution around the average. An IQ of 170 or over would be found in one person in 100,000, whereas 46 people in 100 are of average or near average intelligence.

If talent were a function of intelligence alone, then a definition of exceptional talent might relate to the possession of an IQ of 150 or more, or 1–2 people per 1,000 of the population. This demonstrates clearly the relative scarcity of one of the resources with which this book is concerned.

Gardner[2] sums up current thinking on intelligence testing by asserting that most psychologists are convinced that enthusiasm over intelligence tests has been excessive and that there are numerous limitations in the instruments themselves and in the uses to which they can (and should) be put. Tests are biased in favour of individuals who are accustomed to taking them, and they tend to favour people from particular cultural backgrounds. They have predictive power for success in schooling, but are relatively poor predictors of occupational success, especially when other factors like social and economic background have been taken into account.

This is not the place to try to give a full account of research into the nature and structure of intelligence, which would require a volume in itself, but some reference to it is essential.

There are, indeed, strong differences of opinion among psychologists as to the structure and nature of intelligence. On one side are ranged those who accept the theories of the British psychologist Spearman and believe in the existence of "g", a general overriding factor of intelligence which is measured by every task in an intelligence test. An opposed view is held by followers of the American psychologist Thurstone who believe in the existence of a small set of primary mental faculties which are relatively independent of each other and which are measured by different types of task. Thurstone himself nominated seven factors: verbal comprehension, word fluency, numerical fluency, spatial visualisation, associative memory, perceptual speed and reasoning.

Gardner supports this approach and points out that Piaget – "the theorist of cognitive development" – greatly illuminated the process of intellectual development, valued highly in scientific and philosophical circles, but failed to explain the developmental processes involved in becoming an outstanding lawyer, artist, athlete or political leader.

Among the various approaches to measurement and definition, perhaps the most widely respected work in recent years is that of the American psychologist Guilford.[3]

Guilford's dimensions of intellectual activity. Guilford holds that intelligence is not a unitary variable, but a cluster of very specific intellectual abilities. He found that correlations between different intelligence test scores were often zero, with the implication that they were not measuring the same thing. Using factor analysis he identified three dimensions of intellectual activity. The first is the dimension of operation, which has to do with the way information is processed. It has five sub-groups.

* Cognition
* Memory
* Divergent production (lateral thinking)
* Convergent thinking (inference)
* Evaluation

The second dimension is content, relating to the type of information being processed. This has four categories.

- Figural
- Symbolic
- Semantic
- Behavioural

The final dimension is that of product, which reflects the form of the information after it has been processed. This includes the following.

- Units
- Classes
- Relations
- Systems
- Transformation
- Implications

The practical implications of Guilford's work are far-reaching. For example, even if we confine our definition of talent to the possession of an exceptionally high level of intelligence, there remains enormous scope for identifying different kinds of talent (that is, different kinds of intelligence) and relating these to different kinds of work. Guilford's theories suggest the existence of 120 different types ($5 \times 4 \times 6$).

Gardner's categories of intelligence. Gardner has developed his own theory of the structure of multiple intelligences. His categories are as follows.

- Linguistic
- Musical
- Logical–mathematical
- Spatial
- Bodily–kinaesthetic
- The personal intelligences: knowledge of self and knowledge of others

These categories certainly relate well on a common sense level to the various kinds of talent which are evident in different fields of activity or different occupations.

Linguistic ability is the foundation of the skill of the writer and poet and is seen at its height in the work of Shakespeare. Musical intelligence, shown in the output of composers, vocalists and instrumentalists, is seen in its purest form in Mozart. Logical-mathematic intelligence lies behind the work of the scientist/mathematician, exemplified at the genius level by Einstein. Spatial intelligence shows itself most clearly in the architectural profession, but is a factor in art and design also. Bodily-kinaesthetic intelligence shows itself in dance, athletics and the exercise of craft skills. Finally, the personal intelligences are at work in such fields of activity as politics, therapy, counselling and success as a parent as well as being an important factor in leadership skills.

Some occupations, if they are to be carried out at the level of excellence, call for high levels of ability on several dimensions. The outstanding advocate or attorney, for example, needs high linguistic skills, considerable capability for logical reasoning and highly developed personal skills.

There are well-known cases in which an individual is at or near the genius level on one dimension only and well below average or even subnormal on virtually all the others. This is so in the case of the idiot-savant. An outstanding example discovered in the UK in recent years is Stephen Wiltshire, a 12-year-old boy with very limited educational attainment but with outstanding talent in the field of architectural drawing. He can capture on paper both the detailed features and the overall mass of the most complex structures after a brief spell of observation.

Achievement and non-intellectual factors

In Galton's view the determining factors that lead geniuses to perform great acts of creativity are "capacity, zeal and the tendency to work hard". Much work has been done on what it is that determines achievement from high potential. An important study carried out in the USA in the 1920s[4] followed 1,300 highly gifted children, selected from over 150,000, into adulthood. It showed that giftedness, as measured by intelligence tests, is not necessarily reflected in achievements in later life. The conclusion was that intelligence test scores can predict such things as level of income, marital happiness, health and emotional stability, but not outstanding achievement. Significant achievement in adulthood must, therefore, be attributed largely to non-intellectual factors.

There have been several subsequent studies of famous historical figures (C.M. Cox[5]), eminent scientists (A. Roe[6]) and others of living people of exceptional creativity or achievement such as the work of the Institute for Personality Assessment and Research (IPAR) and Zuckerman's study of the winners of the Nobel prize for science currently living in the USA. The IPAR work was based on particular fields of activity: architecture, scientific research, invention and mathematics. Outstanding people in these fields spent three days living in at the institute being interviewed and tested. R. Ochse[7] has comprehensively surveyed the research evidence which relates to high achievers and creative people; some of her most important findings are set out below.

- They come predominantly from the middle classes and are particularly likely to have had one or both parents in the professions. For example, in Zuckerman's study, 29% of those with science doctorates and 53% of Nobel prizewinners in science came from professional backgrounds compared with 3.5% of US employed males as a whole. There are clearly some environmental (and/or genetic) factors which enhance the possibility that the children of the professional classes will eventually develop into adults capable of outstanding achievements. A professional-class home does not, however, necessarily mean a wealthy one. The various research findings indicate that there is little or no relationship between talent and family wealth.
- Jews are very significantly over-represented, while Catholics are under-represented. Although only 3% of the US population is Jewish, 27% of the Nobel Laureates in Zuckerman's sample were Jewish. None of Roe's 64 leading scientists was Catholic.
- Typically, high achievers tend to be first born or only children. Several investigators have shown that birth order is related to intelligence and a number of studies link the position of being the first child in the family with creativity.
- High achievers had plenty of intellectual stimulation when young, sometimes at the instigation of their parents, but often self-initiated. They tend to read voraciously as children and to find pleasure or even excitement in intellectual pursuits which other children do their best to avoid. Bertrand Russell described his introduction to Euclid as "one of the great events of my life, as dazzling as first love".
- They were encouraged to place a high value on intellectual achievement. Roe found that learning was greatly valued and pursued for

its own sake in the homes of practically all her highly creative subjects.

- The IPAR studies were among several to find that it was quite common among high achievers to have suffered traumatic experiences when young, like brutality, abuse, frustration and deprivation. Such findings are in conflict with the theories of Rogers, Adler and Rank that to become a creative person you must have loving supporting parents and a happy home environment. Also the incidence of ugliness, deformity or disease was found to be high.
- A disproportionate number of high achievers lost at least one parent in childhood. 26% of Roe's sample of scientists lost a parent before the age of 16. This is three times greater than the parental loss of the US population in general. 30% of Cox's historical geniuses also lost one parent in childhood.
- Social isolation and loneliness also feature strongly in the early lives of the great. Ochse quotes Winston Churchill: "Solitary trees, if they grow at all, grow strong."
- High achievers were frequently subject to strict and stern discipline as children, and often treated cruelly or unfairly.

Defining creativity

For many people the concept of talent has more to do with creativity – the capacity for originality, innovation and discovery – than with intelligence. Creativity in turn has been the subject of almost as much research as intelligence. Guilford has worked in this field as well.[8] He interpreted creativity as problem-solving ability and concluded from his studies that this quality also involves a number of separate abilities.

- Sensitivity to problems.
- Fluency of three kinds: ideational: the ability to generate ideas rapidly; associational: the ability to form associations; expressional: the ability to articulate ideas.
- Flexibility, including: spontaneous flexibility; adaptive flexibility.
- Originality

These concepts form the basis of a test battery for assessing creativity which was developed by Torrance and is in widespread use. Guilford's work is not without its critics and several psychologists have pointed out that there is usually only a very weak correlation between scores on tests based on his ideas and various criteria of creative achievement by adults.

It is interesting to compare Guilford's approach with the description of the creative process offered by the technical director of a UK software engineering business.

> "In my own creative processes intuitions arrive as metaphors or linkages from other fields, crossing boundaries and languages, discovering underlying relationships; being creative without necessarily being original. I take a personal interest in a wide range of disciplines and environments, learning new things, stimulating and sparking off new ideas and solutions. It is so important to be open to ideas outside one's field. There is too much tunnel vision in the management of organisations."

A study of creativity in R&D laboratories[9] listed the personal qualities of creative scientists in order of the frequency with which they were mentioned in 120 interviews.

- Intrinsic motivation: being excited by the work itself and the challenge of the problem.
- Ability and experience: having special problem-solving abilities and skills; having expertise in the particular field of research; having broad general knowledge and experience in several fields; being highly intelligent.
- Risk orientation: being unafraid to take risks.
- Social skills: being a good listener and team member.
- Other qualities: persistence, curiosity, energy and intellectual honesty.

It is well known that Freud attributed creative achievement to the sublimation of energy generated by instinctual drives, particularly the libido, and their direction into creative work.

Ochse points out, however, that Adler and Rank rejected the idea of the sublimation of the sex drive and saw creative output as the result of a positive drive to improve the self and gain mental health. Rank argued that people have to contend with two opposing anxieties: fear of life and fear of death. The former involves fear of separation, first traumatically experienced at the moment of birth. In life it is experienced as a fear of being isolated and alone, giving rise to a need for comfort and security and to depend on more powerful individuals; hence the attractions of belonging to a great and powerful organisation. The fear of death, on the other hand, is the fear of becoming enmeshed with others, of renouncing freedom and individuality, of being controlled by others and dependent on them. This gives rise to a need for self-assertion, autonomy and self-expression and hence to frustration and dissatisfaction with life in an organisation.

Rank's concept of the ideal personality in relation to achievement is one in which these twin fears are balanced. These people accept discipline while preserving their individuality.

Maslow[10] developed the idea of self-actualisation, a drive to develop a person's full potential once lower order needs are satisfied. In his early work Maslow held to the view that true creativity and outstanding achievements were spontaneous, easy, free-flowing and characterised by a lack of effort. At the end of his life he acknowledged the role of "plain hard work" in worthwhile achievements.

A later and very inclusive view of creativity holds that there is no fundamental difference between the creative processes involved in painting a picture, composing a symphony, devising new instruments of killing, developing a scientific theory, or discovering new processes in human relationships or new aspects of an individual's own personality. Central to Carl Rogers's[11] theory of the development of creativity in the individual is the idea that if "conditions of worth" are imposed on children they will incorporate their parents' values into their own value systems. If parents make children feel unworthy for failure to comply with their wishes then children will tend to modify their behaviour in order to conform with their parents' wishes. They will develop defensive attitudes and value their own experience in terms of how far it will lead to an enhanced evaluation of their worth in the eyes of their parents.

Rogers argued, therefore, that creativity is most likely to find expression in people who are fully open to experience and who do not deny or repress what they are feeling. Strong parental values imposed on the child inhibit this process. The development of the kind of healthy, self-actualising personality Rogers believed to be related to creativity depends on the absence of imposed "conditions of worth" and evaluation processes of the kind associated with traditional formal education.

The Gestalt school of psychology holds that people have a natural tendency to organise what they perceive into wholes or "gestalts". The relations between the associated parts of a range of stimuli endow the whole with greater significance than the sum of the individual components. Thus we can recognise a face, a theme from a Beethoven symphony or an aircraft type without being conscious of the particular features or details which go to make up the whole. Creativity can be explained as the process of organising knowledge into gestalts; Wertheimer[12] describes a problem awaiting solution as an incomplete structure or bad gestalt, giving rise to intellectual tension and frustration. The tension sets up a drive to find a solution to the problem which makes possible some kind of harmony or balance between the parts. The creative process is one which destroys a bad gestalt and replaces it with a better one. This involves reorganising existing items of knowledge and ideas into a new internally consistent pattern or paradigm.

Ochse points out that many of the characteristics of creative people are also characteristic of leaders and other high achievers and that these qualities predict achievement in general rather than creativity as such. She quotes research by Cox, however, which does highlight some differences. Leaders scored much more highly than creators on the following items.

- Working or playing for the group rather than own advantage.
- Tendency to do their duty rather than follow personal inclination.
- Forcefulness or strength of character.
- Widespread influence.

Other findings on creativity

Precocity. Research findings suggest that creativity in later life is often foreshadowed by precocity in childhood.

The link between creativity and intelligence. Creativity tends to require a minimum level of mental ability; however, above a certain level of intelligence there appears to be no firm relationship between creativity and intelligence other than in the possession of specific abilities or aptitudes.

Psychopathology. There is considerable evidence that the incidence of psychopathology is higher among creative people than in the population as a whole.

Ochse hypothesises that the link between creative output and the pathological personality may be a motivational thrust, resulting from emotional insecurity, which has two possible consequences: creative activity and emotional or behavioural disorder.

Studies of the personality of creative individuals do suggest that typically they are emotionally unstable and impulsive, although this tendency is more pronounced among creative people in the arts than in the sciences. Cox, for example, found depression and anger to be common characteristics of creative people.

To balance such weaknesses, however, the evidence suggests that they are able to control their emotions when needed and that in one area of life at least they are well adjusted and happy – in their work.

Aesthetic values. All types of creative persons studied by the IPAR researchers, not just those in the arts, scored highly on tests measuring aesthetic values, and biographies reveal that scientists and artists found deep satisfaction in the aesthetic aspects of their work. The outstanding British aeronautical engineer, Sir Barnes Wallis, saw creative engineering as an art and himself as a kind of poet.

Sexual orientation. Studies of sexual orientation show that many historical and contemporary persons of outstanding creative output were or are homosexually inclined, and that they are less likely than the general population to be happily married or married at all.

Independence. A salient characteristic is emotional and intellectual independence; creative people tend to be autonomous and self-sufficient, non-conforming, unconventional or even rebellious. At the same time they display self-confidence and have insight into their own creative powers.

A commonly identified trait of the truly creative person is a preference for, and habit of, working alone. Ochse quotes case after case where this was so: from Byron to Schlesinger, from Gibbon to Wagner and from Edison to Voltaire. The latter, in order to complete Candide, locked himself up for three days, opening the door only to take in his meals. Goethe declared "I cannot produce the least thing without absolute loneliness."

This characteristic points to the source of one of the major problems involved when industry employs creative people. The nature of much innovation in industry, because of the scale of the work to be undertaken and because much of it needs to be interdisciplinary, is such that the requirement is for people who work well as members of teams.

Research findings support the view that creativity is the preserve of the lonely. People tend to produce better ideas when on their own and nominal groups (involving a number of individuals working separately) produce better ideas than do the same number of people interacting in a problem-solving team.

This places a high premium on the skills of management and team leadership in those situations where teamwork is, for one reason or another, essential.

SUMMARY

The essence of talent is extraordinariness linked to individuality. Highly gifted people stand out. They experience being different from an early age, whether or not their exceptional abilities are recognised.

Although the existence of extraordinary ability has been acknowledged throughout history, systematic and scientific steps to study its nature and origins date from relatively recent times. The work of Francis Galton marks the beginning of the period during which talent has been rigorously investigated.

Talent is closely identified with intelligence and techniques for the measurement of intelligence have developed considerably over the years. Measures show a bell-shaped distribution around the average 100, with 1–2 people in 1,000 scoring over 150. Recent theories stress the many-sided nature of intelligence, whereas earlier emphasis was largely on verbal and mathematical/logical ability.

Many studies have shown, however, that gifted children do not necessarily fulfil early promise by outstanding achievements in later life. Studies of historical figures of outstanding talent and of contemporary high achievers have emphasised the considerable importance of non-intellectual factors in determining whether or not latent ability is made manifest in the individual's life's work.

The emphasis has switched from intelligence to creativity as the key underlying characteristic linked to achievement, particularly in such fields as scientific research. Yet creativity has turned out to be a more complex, more elusive concept than intelligence.

Measurements of creativity characteristically have low predictive validity and there are widely divergent theories about the factors which nourish it.

Standing out from the enormous bank of theory and research is a general view of what is meant by talent. It is the possession and application of outstanding ability in one or more specified fields.

- Verbal or linguistic activity.
- Mathematical and/or logical reasoning.
- Music.
- Spatial perception.

- Social and interpersonal behaviour.

In each of these fields the extra ingredients – the ones that make the difference – are what we call creativity in the sense of approaches which are original, inventive and novel, along with a range of personal qualities.

References

1 Francis Galton, *Hereditary Genius*, New York, Appleton, 1869.
2 Howard Gardner, *Frames of Mind: The Theory of Multiple Intelligences*, London, Heinemann, 1983.
3 J.P. Guilford, *The Nature of Human Intelligence*, New York, McGraw Hill, 1967.
4 L.M. Terman, *Mental and physical traits of a thousand gifted children*, Stanford, Stanford University Press, 1925.
5 C.M. Cox, *The early mental traits of three hundred geniuses*, Stanford, Stanford University Press, 1926.
6 A. Roe, "A psychologist examines sixty four eminent scientists" in P.E. Vernon (ed.), *Creativity: Selected Readings*, Harmondsworth, Penguin, 1970.
7 R. Ochse, *Before the Gates of Excellence*, Cambridge, Cambridge University Press, 1990.
8 J.P. Guilford, "Creativity: a quarter of a century of progress" in I.A. Taylor and J.W. Getzels (eds), *Perspectives in Creativity*, Chicago, Aldine Publishing Company, 1975.
9 Teresa M. Amabile and Stanley S. Gryskiewicz, *Creativity in the R&D Laboratory*, Technical Report 30, Greensboro N.C., Center for Creative Leadership, 1987.
10 A. Maslow, *Motivation and Personality*, New York, Harper, 1954.
11 Carl Rogers, "Toward a theory of creativity" in A. Rothenberg and C.R. Hausman (eds), The *Creativity Question*, Durham N.C., Duke University Press, 1976.
12 M. Wertheimer, *Productive Thinking*, New York, Harper and Row, 1945.

3

TALENT REDEFINED BY BUSINESS

"Intelligence is . . . accuracy, ease in learning; ability to grasp quickly
the point of view of the commanding officer, to issue clear and
intelligent orders, to estimate a new situation and to arrive at a
sensible decision in a crisis."

US Army, Officer Rating Scale, 1919

The lack of a strong correlation between intelligence and academic
attainment and career achievement has been established by research
studies of the kind described in the preceding chapter. Practitioners in
organisations have increasingly observed the same lack of correlation.
This applies equally to the careers of highly qualified specialists, and
those recruited more specifically for their level of general mental ability
(like entrants to the highest grades in the UK Civil Service, or those
selected as potential general managers).

Meanwhile the organisations themselves have been changing,
responding in turn to changes in technology, in competitive pressures,
and in peoples' attitudes and expectations. These forces have led to
marked shifts in the roles that those in senior positions are being called
upon to play. Traditional authority, whether that of the expert specialist or the authoritarian manager, has increasingly been challenged.
Consistency of thought and behaviour has had to give way to flexibility
of attitude and adaptive behaviour. To succeed in the complex yet subtle processes of influence and decision-making in modern organisations
people have had to acquire new skills and display additional qualities.
Words like leadership, creativity, interpersonal skills, communication,
commitment, drive, initiative and entrepreneurial skills are increasingly to be found appearing in person specifications in selection briefs.

The new corporate requirements

In one large European international business, the talented individual
was defined as one who:

- knows the business, the products and the markets;
- is extremely good at communication;
- has a "winner's mentality";
- has drive;
- is able to operate in an ambiguous environment;
- has not just intelligence but "social intelligence", being able to understand human processes, political processes, bargaining processes;
- can take initiative and sensible risks.

The response of a UK merchant bank to the question "How do you define talent?" was "intelligent, bright team players capable of progressing and growing".

A French company specified "people who are creative, adaptable, ambitious for themselves; who are courageous and assertive; open-minded people who think in an international way".

Peter Drucker[1] points out that, nevertheless, no educational establishment – in his opinion not even the business schools – tries to equip students with the skills needed to become effective in business organisations, such as the ability to present ideas orally and in writing and the ability to work with people.

A vice-president of Rockwell, reflecting on 30 years' experience, pointed out that when someone had to be removed from a position, 95% of the time the reason was not any lack of technical competency or understanding of the job. It was their inability to get things done, to take leadership and get the commitment of the organisation behind them. The educational system provided a grounding in how to think and how to analyse a problem, "But how do the educational institutions prepare individuals that have to go into the workplace and work with live examples . . . we don't prepare the student in the classroom for these types of things".

It is clear then that talent can no longer be adequately defined in terms of intellectual gifts or specific vocational aptitudes, or abilities of the kind that go with being an outstandingly able engineer, scientist, actuary or advocate. These qualities may be necessary in the make-up of high achievers but by themselves they are not sufficient to guarantee it. The additional, non-intellectual qualities which contribute as much, if not more, to success must, therefore, be identified, defined with precision and accurately assessed or measured.

It is at this point that the difficulties involved in managing talent begin. Whereas intelligence can be precisely (if somewhat tautologically) defined as that attribute which intelligence tests measure, and academic attainment is signified by the traditional benchmarks of academic distinction built into various national education systems, there is far less consensus concerning the precise nature of these other personal qualities. Ask any 20 top executives in the human resources field to define leadership, for example, and you will get 20 different answers.

There are, however, methodological problems of considerable difficulty, beyond questions of definition. There is the fact that the qualities which were associated with success in the past will not necessarily be associated with success in the future. Alvin Toffler[2] pointed out that it is not the incompetent people who destroy great organisations; they rarely get into positions of power in sufficient numbers. Organisations are destroyed more often by highly competent people who, once they reach positions of power, fail to perceive the need for change and cling to practices and procedures long after they have ceased to be relevant in the new environment for business. Attempts to identify the qualities needed by tomorrow's elites on the basis of identifying the qualities displayed by the elites of today and yesterday may, therefore, be doomed to failure.

In any case it is dangerous to assume that the qualities associated with effectiveness in contributing to organisational achievement can be inferred from analysing the qualities of those who have advanced through the traditional hierarchies of organisations over the past 20–30 years. There are many reasons why people may achieve steady promotion other than the possession of exceptional talent, including time-serving in organisations which reward loyalty and seniority, conformity in organisations which reject the eccentric or the unusual, keeping their noses clean in organisations which are risk-averse, or simply just fitting in well in organisations with strong cultures.

The more sophisticated large organisations are well aware of these problems. What differentiates them is the degree of confidence they display in their ability, nevertheless, to define clearly and validly the qualities they are looking for and the extent to which they have developed elaborate systems and procedures to help them do so.

The categories of talent

A pragmatic way of defining the people this book is about is to say that they are the people who are, or who one day will be, on the files of the search agencies or of companies directly competing with their own. There is a whole world of intelligence gathering of which the individual becomes aware the first time he or she answers the telephone to find a headhunter with an invitation to lunch at the other end of the line.

There are four main categories of talent sought after by business organisations.

1 Talent in the form of specialist expertise or skill

Business organisations need to employ actuaries, accountants, architects, designers, engineers, scientists, software writers and experts of many other kinds. These are the core roles of the talent-intensive organisation. Architectural practices are built around architects, legal firms around lawyers, computer firms around hardware and software engineers, pharmaceutical firms around research scientists and airlines around pilots.

Several companies which primarily define talent in terms of specialist expertise qualify their requirements by adding additional attributes in the area of personal qualities.

In GEC-ALSTHOM, for example, although the quest is for people with good vocational skills and experience (90% of the recruits are engineers), other attributes are equally important.

> "They must have a very strong basis in their own field and they must be technically competent. They have to be very involved in their work and efficient. They must be innovative, creative and broad-thinking. They must be people who like to change, who enjoy challenge and mobility, and who are open and communicative in relation to the environment and to other people."

British Airways is looking for people who are "qualified, technically and professionally, but who also have leadership qualities and interpersonal skills. The latter are critical for success".

Bayer looks for an excellent base for talent in the form of an excellent degree or excellent vocational training.

> "We are looking for social skills as well. Therefore we look, at entry level, for people that have some extra experience that goes beyond the traditional degree; have they been involved, for example, in student or youth activities? Have they travelled? Do they have international experience or languages? Things that show a particular personality, a kind of openness we are looking for."

In most instances such recruits can be expected to be productive relatively shortly after joining the organisation, particularly if they have some previous experience as well as being qualified. Different kinds of expertise can be expected to attain peak performance at different age/experience points. In some cases the first few years after joining may well be the most productive, due to such factors as the possession of the most up-to-date professional knowledge, the peaking of certain mental or physical abilities in the early 20s or sheer energy and enthusiasm. In others performance will improve steadily with maturity and experience. In nearly every case, however, it is anticipated that the individual being recruited is in a real sense qualified to do the job (as well as being qualified on paper) and will very quickly become effective. The exceptions are those (such as airline pilots) where the specialist qualification is achieved after entry to the organisation. Thus most specialist personnel are recruited on the basis of what they are rather than what their potential is. Given that they have qualified in their respective fields it is taken for granted that they possess the relevant abilities, knowledge and skills which will equip them to practise within a relatively short space of time. The other categories of talent described below are different in that, in as far as recruitment focuses on young people, they are being recruited primarily for their potential rather than for their qualifications.

2 Talent in the form of ability to manage and lead

Business organisations cannot survive without an adequate supply of talented managers. In the talent-intensive organisation these can be drawn from two sources: from the ranks of those with specialist expertise; or from a pool of talent recruited specifically for their management potential (in the case of young people) or a proven managerial track record (in the case of experienced personnel). The Prudential Corporation, for example, drew virtually all its managers from the ranks of its actuarial and professional specialists until the early 1980s, since when it has followed the alternative course of recruiting specifically for management potential.

In the recruitment of young potential managers a common assumption is that the knowledge and skills required to operate effectively as a manager will be acquired over time as a consequence of a mixture of experience and management development programmes. The selection decision is based, therefore, on judgments about the personal qualities likely to be associated with future success as a manager. These will include such attributes as intelligence, energy, analytical ability, oral communication and the like. "We are looking at people who are entrepreneurial in outlook, probably charismatic, who have an international orientation, who are comfortable in a number of languages, are numerate and creative."

An alternative approach more favoured by some US firms, and particularly so by management consultants and Wall Street firms, is to recruit "ready made" managers in the form of MBA graduates; particularly those from the most prestigious business schools such as Harvard, MIT, Stanford or Northwestern.

Closely associated with management is what is perhaps the rarest talent of all: leadership ability. This can be defined as the ability to develop a vision of some future state, articulate that vision for others, persuade them to share it and inspire them to work towards its achievement.

Some, but by no means all, organisations look for leadership potential in their young recruits. They are most likely to do so when recruiting young entrants to a management training scheme and least likely to do so when recruiting specialists.

The process of specifying the qualities associated with leadership potential is undoubtedly the most difficult and most controversial aspect of the identification of talent.

Donald McKinnon[3] of the University of California in a paper presented to a conference on creativity specified no fewer than 21 qualities or traits which in his view contributed to overall performance in the leadership of people engaged in creative activity. These were as follows.

- Effective intelligence, which McKinnon defines as the ability to solve problems in a way which leads to practical action.
- Breadth of interests, including ones outside business.
- Perception of problems as challenges or as offering scope for change and improvement.
- Effectiveness in organising and planning both their own work and that of others.
- Ability to make clear firm decisions under pressure.
- Originality.
- Practical judgment.
- Flexibility.
- Listening skills.
- Oral communication skills.
- Written communication skills.
- Presence or charisma.
- Personal warmth.

- A tendency to seek and find acceptance in a leading role in a group.
- Responsibility and willingness to accept the consequences of their own actions.
- Maturity and emotional stability.
- Personal courage.
- Achievement motivation.
- Energy and stamina.
- Resistance to stress.
- Sense of humour.

The list may or may not be valid. The problem lies in devising an economic and valid process for assessing such a range of qualities for selection purposes.

3 Business-getting talent

Organisations which exist to exploit human knowledge and skill have found it increasingly necessary to search out those whose special talents lie in the field of business-getting, whether they are called marketing personnel, sales representatives, account executives, agents or whatever. These are people who on the one hand are capable of understanding quite complex products such as financial instruments or computers yet whose main value to the organisation is their ability to promote and sell them. Here, too, the youngest recruits are brought in for their potential, trained and developed and tested in practice before they are expected to reach peak performance.

In some cases the business-getters have low status; in others they are the elite. In IBM, for example, the sales function is the quickest and surest route to the top. IBM's sales trainees get one year's initial training: nine months in the field at a branch and three months in one of IBM's National Education Centres. A training manager at the branch will supervise each trainee's programme which will include self-paced learning modules ranging from the company's culture and values to basic product knowledge. Trainees accompany experienced staff making company calls. They make their first product demonstration before a critical group of experienced representatives. At the education centre learning to sell begins on the second day of the course. The syllabus covers the company's support structure and how to use it, an analysis of the competition and an introduction to business skills.

Whereas many companies give the task of training new sales people to their least productive or "burned out" sales staff, IBM believes that the sales force is far too important for its training to be left to mediocre people. It employs its top sales staff as instructors.

4 Hybrid talent

The fourth category of talent is the "hybrid"; the individual who is seen as having the potential to perform two of these roles with more than usual success. In talent-intensive organisations the most wanted but most elusive "hybrid" is the scientist capable of doing exceptionally creative work who also has the potential to manage, not just the R&D laboratory, but the business as a whole, or the software engineer in the mould of Bill Hewlett and Dave Packard, capable not only of developing highly innovative technology but also of building a global business.

How companies use the categories of talent

Companies differ greatly in the extent to which they differentiate these four categories of talent. At one extreme lies the company (exemplified by Sotheby's in the UK) which basically recruits specialists (in this case fine art experts) and hopes to develop at least a reasonable proportion of them to become business-getters and line managers. In practice each fine art or decorative arts expert department tends to have a "hybrid" as manager – that is, a person who manages, exercises leadership, gets the business and is an expert in his or her own field – and two or three others, some purely specialist, others who combine specialist knowledge with business-getting skills. There is no place, however, in the expert department for the person with business-getting skills alone.

At the other extreme lies the company (IBM is a good example) where the roles are relatively distinct. There are managers, specialists in systems or research or software, and the sales force.

For the British Broadcasting Corporation the core talent consists of the creative people; the presenters, writers, producers, directors, camera people and so on. Traditionally the BBC has trained and developed its own and has acted as the training ground for much of the rest of the UK broadcasting, television and video industry. Traditionally, too, most of the managers emerged from their ranks. In the 1950s and 1960s, when management was more to do with systems, procedures and authority, it was all right for ex-programme makers to become managers with little or no preparation for the role. It is a less appropriate route today since management has become much more a profession, demanding high standards of competence. Until relatively recently programme-making was seen as creative and exciting in contrast to management, which was seen as tedious, bureaucratic and boring. This is changing; nowadays management is more likely to be seen as a creative, challenging activity.

In the leading UK design consultancy Coley Porter Bell, business-getting is seen as a key factor in the firm's success. Although designers are seen as vitally important it remains the case that in this company the top person is a marketing specialist. No designers have crossed the divide and become full-time business-getters, although some designers have developed the skills. The view at the top is that designers often lack business skills.

In Harlow Butler Ueda, the leading UK money broker, there is no distinction made. Young people are recruited to be trained as dealers. They are also expected to act as business-getters. "The marketing side is quite important – the relationships are vital." The best brokers are then the ones who have traditionally moved up via desk leader to higher management positions.

EMI Music – now arguably the world's biggest producer of recorded popular music – recognises the need for good marketing and good management, but in this company there is no doubt at all that the key talent for competitive success is the possession of "golden ears", namely the ability to recognise the kind of sound that will get young people rushing to the record stores. The small number of "Artists and Repertoire" personnel who find and nourish the pop stars are often the ones with the highest status and the highest rewards.

The current trend appears increasingly to favour the cultivation of hybrids. Hammond and Holton[4] quote research by Bournois and Chauchat which involved interviews with 40 human-resource directors and CEOs. They found that 60% considered "double training" in engineering and management important. This was particularly so in global businesses such as Philips, SmithKline Beecham, Thomson and Henkel. There was more attention to this in France and Germany than in other European companies.

Esso has invested substantially in training programmes to cross skills between IT managers and those in other functions and now nearly every project has a hybrid manager involved. According to Ian Glenday, Esso's IT manager, the results are evident: "Today nearly 90% of projects are delivered on time and within budget compared with 60% several years ago."

How common are the talented hybrids? Does it make sense to base a human-resource strategy on plans to develop them in sufficient numbers to meet all conceivable needs? Or will they form a minority with most managerial and business-getting positions filled by non-specialists? John Ockenden, chairman of the UK's Data Logic, clearly feels that the truly talented hybrid is so rare as to make it unlikely that the talent-intensive organisation will be able to develop the managers and business-getters it needs from the ranks of its specialists.

He has had long experience of managing technical specialists in software and systems. He still finds them difficult to manage. The problem as he sees it is to make them more free-thinking, less task-oriented. They need imagination and flair. They want job pride, not power or money.

> "Not many of them get to the top, mainly because they don't want to. They don't fully acknowledge that customers come first. They want to give them what they think they ought to have. They don't always accept that intellectual compromise is necessary. I believe passionately in leadership but it is a rare quality in this business. They are not typically charismatic people but rather hard-working, meritocratic, grammar-school types."

Similarly, a director of Coley Porter Bell, a person with a marketing background, considered that the biggest issue facing the company was that creative people functioned in different ways from the managers and the business-getters; they had different priorities, namely to achieve creative perfection. The problem was how to achieve the right balance. She added that over time she had learned to see their side but that, bluntly, she had been helped by the recession. Designers were now actually asking: "Is my job profitable?"

Keith Bedell-Pearce, chief executive of Prudential Financial Services takes a different view.

> "Beneath the surface the qualities that make a good specialist are not that different from those needed for general management. Professionals need to grasp technical knowledge, synthesise, analyse and communicate. Technically brilliant people are usually competent salespersons of their ideas. They also need a strong disciplined approach, using 'process', and scientific method. They do need training in interpersonal skills and a repertoire of styles when dealing with large numbers."

The search for the specialist plus

To sum up, the core talent of the talent-intensive business is the specialist knowledge or skill around which the business is built. Life insurance is built around actuarial science, the computer industry is built around electronics engineering, the software industry around programming. The needs of business are such, however, that the value of the pure specialist is limited. To be fully effective in business (as distinct from, for example, the academic world or parts of the public sector) specialists need other qualities besides those which are implied by their professional qualifications. As a minimum they need to be able to communicate effectively with their non-technical colleagues and, in many cases, with the firm's customers. They need to understand the nature of business, the need for profit, the importance of deadlines and to acknowledge the imperatives of the market place. So the search is not just for the most highly qualified specialists; it is a search for the specialist plus, people with qualities which enable them to fit in well in the framework of the business organisation. The specification for the "hybrid" was well put by the spokesman for Continental AG.

"So you can see the characteristics of the talented person are emerging from this context. We need very well functionally-trained, educated individuals. Good chemists, good commercial people, good mechanical engineers, and so on. Secondly we need real talent in extra-functional skills like communication and the management of people, how to inspire with a particular vision and to follow that direction. We need people who are able, besides producing short-term results, to keep the strategic view and to act on it. But the functional expertise – being grounded with an understanding of those skills – is very important and we must not lose sight of the importance of that. Then there is the ability to handle uncertainty and ambiguity and speed of change. All we know about the future points to more of that. But it is not what German people like; they do not feel happy in those situations. Now we need the ability to handle that to be characteristic of our managers, plus they need to be able to communicate in the international arena."

The business also needs the functions of management and marketing to be carried out superbly well, and in most cases it is discovered that really first-class managers and marketing people are actually at least as rare as first-class specialists. At the same time they do not come armed with certificates of competence, not even if they have MBA degrees or Advanced Marketing Diplomas. It is reasonably safe to assume that a recently qualified doctor is capable of practising his or her profession to a generally accepted level of competence. No such assumption can be made on the basis of an MBA qualification. The search, then, is for those with the potential to excel in management and marketing.

Beyond this is the search for that rare talent – leadership – for those, in particular, who are capable of rising to chief executive positions and who will, in the fullness of time, hold the destiny of the enterprise in their hands.

In the case of some organisations the strategic approach is to recruit talent for the core specialists and to endeavour to develop managerial, marketing and business skills among at least a significant number of them; this is the "hybrid" approach. In other cases the streams of talent are kept much more distinct, albeit with some opportunities for crossing over, with separate recruiting and development programmes for managerial, marketing and specialist personnel and sometimes with a fourth "high flyer" or "crown prince" stream for tomorrow's top level leaders.

The strongest argument for developing hybrids is that they can build bridges within organisations between the sub-cultures of business management with its bottom line focus, the business-getting group with its customer focus and the technologists with their professional focus. They can ensure business plans are based on sound technological judgment and can focus research and development on business goals.

Every personnel director's dream is the articulate scientist, fluent in the language of business, respected by their technical and non-technical peers alike, superbly competent at selling their company's products or services and destined by virtue of their charisma and vision to end their career as the chief executive of a major enterprise. If people with very high IQs constitute one in 1,000 then those with even reasonably high IQs and all the other qualities which go with the virtues listed above will occur naturally at an even lower incidence. Do we have to wait for them to appear and rise to the top as corks rise to the surface of water, or can we build on potential and develop talent of this kind and make it multiply?

New sources of talent

Traditionally, the kinds of highly educated scientific, professional and technical talent employed by talent-intensive businesses in such fields as electronic engineering, chemicals, financial and business services have been drawn from the male population and from indigenous populations with dominant ethnic majorities.

This situation is changing rapidly and for several reasons.

- Legislation and public pressure against discrimination in employ-ment have obviously become important influences. The BBC, for example, has stated its intention to reflect in its workforce the ethnic composition of the nation it serves.
- The scarcity of talent in key areas – software engineering is a notice-able example – has forced companies to look outside their traditional sources of recruits.
- In so doing they have discovered very high levels of ability and apti-tude. People from Asian minorities for example, have excelled in the field of software writing. This field has also proved a successful one for women, as has financial services.
- The discovery that "what makes a company creative is the multiplic-ity of the origins of their people". This is the view taken, for example, by L'Oréal in France.

> "Their nationality; their race; their culture; their education also. Again in marketing you might imagine that it is better to have people with *grande école* qualifications, say, in marketing or economics, but we say no. It is good to have people who have studied at the London School of Economics or the London Business School or INSEAD, but if you have only those people you won't have such a good marketing department. It will be too homogeneous. So we have to enrich our creativity with people who have been studying history, or literature, or law, and so on.
>
> We also want to bring up women to top jobs. For instance, we have 160 young women around the world who are on the top directive committees in our subsidiaries, in posts such as marketing director, or sales director, or financial director. We have a young woman who is working in the UK and is in charge of L'Oréal there, not the whole company, but a large part of it called L'Oréal Parfumer. She is the managing director, she is French and she is 33."

SUMMARY

The view of talent taken by industry and commerce has developed in response to the interaction of experience of success and failure in recruiting on the one hand, and changes in the demands made upon talented people in their various roles on the other.

The lack of correlation between intelligence and academic attainment and career success has become increasingly evident. At the same time social changes, such as the increasing tendency to challenge the traditional sources of authority, have led to important shifts in the qualities required for effective management and for the successful carrying out of professional and technical roles.

The educational systems of the advanced countries have, however, been slow to respond to such changes. There is little provision in educational institutions for equipping students with the key skills they will require in business.

If it is no longer adequate to define talent in terms of intelligence and academic attainment and other, non-intellectual qualities, are seen as vital components, there is a need for a new, more precise language and set of definitions with which to specify the nature of the talent that is required. No such language exists.

Other difficulties are to do with the problem of trying to specify the qualities required to perform effectively in an unknown and uncertain future, using evidence and role models derived from the past.

Business organisations seek four main types of talent: specialists, managers, business-getters and "hybrids".

In talent-intensive organisations hybrids are the most prized assets since they can bridge sub-cultures, ensure business decisions are illuminated by technical knowledge and ensure technical effort is closely harnessed to business objectives.

Can hybrids be developed? Opinions on this differ, but considering their value it is clearly worth trying, and more and more organisations are doing so.

References

1 Peter Drucker, *Managing for the Future*, Oxford, Butterworth Heinemann, 1992.
2 Alvin Toffler, *The Adaptive Corporation*, Aldershot, Gower, 1985.
3 Donald McKinnon, "Designing an Assessment Centre for Creative Leaders in the 1980s", in S. Gryskiewicz *et al.* (eds), *Selected Readings in Creativity*, vol.1, Greensboro N.C., Centre for Creative Leadership, 1981.
4 Valerie Hammond and Viki Holton, *Information Technology Environments*, Berkhamsted, Ashridge Management Research Group, 1991.

4

RECRUITING THE MOST TALENTED

"We seek people who want to make a difference. We are building an organisation that will make a difference on a global scale. We commit ourselves to create a corporate culture which will attract and nurture those individuals who can and want to make a difference."

SRI International, California, USA

Why companies seek out exceptional talent

Companies look for talent, in the simplest terms, for what it can do. Design agencies want the best designers, software houses the best software writers, organisations of all kinds want the best managers. Companies also recruit exceptionally talented people for their potential, for what it is hoped they will do in the future. This rationale has two distinct aspects: one is to ensure an adequate future supply of high level talent; the other is a recognition that tomorrow's best practice in any particular field may well be radically different from today's. This latter aspect may be critically important in such fields as design where the rate and scale of change in taste and acceptable imagery between one generation and the next is very marked.

Another reason is more to do with marketing than output. The acquisition of talented personnel who are "names" in their field adds to the reputation of an organisation and can be powerful in attracting clients on the one hand (talented individuals frequently have their own personal following) and yet more talented recruits on the other.

Closely related to this objective is the attitude: "Only the best are good enough for us." This can mean trouble; organisations outstanding in their fields and with reputations such that they are able to be highly selective among applicants often accept only those who can demonstrate exceptional talent, irrespective of any consideration of how many exceptionally talented people of what kinds are actually needed. This results in the recruiting of people who are overqualified for the tasks they can be assigned to, and who then experience dissatisfaction, frustration and disillusion.

Reasons for not recruiting exceptionally talented people

Not all organisations set out to recruit top talent. Those which do not may hold back for a variety of reasons. The most common, although the least likely to be publicly acknowledged, is feelings of inferiority on the part of those currently in positions of power who are afraid that they might be overshadowed and, indeed, overtaken by persons clearly more capable than themselves. This attitude has lain behind the lack of enthusiasm in the past on the part of many UK companies for graduate recruitment. It persists today in a frequently expressed mistrust of candidates with first class honours degrees who are supposedly "too clever by half" and those with MBA degrees who are supposedly "arrogant".

There is also a genuine belief that in the particular field in which the company operates teamwork is more vital to success than individual excellence, with the result that selection criteria focus on the ability to contribute to team-working rather than on individual excellence. This approach is exemplified by the behaviour of some soccer club managers who instead of trying to buy star players in the transfer market concentrate on team-building with relatively unknown players, usually recruited locally, initially as apprentices.

Companies can also believe that the price is too high; that exceptionally talented people demand too much. This may not only reflect a view that they have priced themselves out of the market in purely financial terms but also the feeling that they demand too much in the way of attention, special privileges and "stroking". This is also commonly given in the UK as a reason for not recruiting MBAs.

A particular philosophy, best described as anti-elitist, holds the view that there is enormous latent talent in the workforce, especially among people who have been deprived of educational opportunities, and that the first priority is to identify, develop and grow talent from the shop floor upwards rather than seek it on the outside. This attitude has been a strong tradition in the UK police, for example.

Alternative approaches to recruiting talent

There are two extreme approaches to recruiting the necessary supply of fresh talent.

- The first is what Randall[1] has called the "agricultural" method, which to extend the metaphor involves acquiring high quality seed material with growth potential, planting the young entrants in a supportive environment, nurturing and developing them and weeding out those who do not "take". This process, known in industry as "growing your own", was the principal, but not the exclusive, source of talent in most companies involved in this study.

- The second, what Randall calls the "purchasing" method, involves buying the talent ready-made, usually by employing headhunters.

Between the extremes lies the case in which people with a small amount of experience are sought out with the intention of getting the best of both worlds: acquiring personnel already to some extent guaranteed, but who can still be moulded and adapted to the company culture.

The particular approach adopted by a company will relate to a number of factors, including tradition, rate of growth and current competition in the labour market. Often the development of new technologies or moves into new business areas or markets create a demand for skills not previously required with a consequent need to recruit experienced personnel from outside. Kleinwort Benson, for example, was traditionally almost exclusively a "grow your own" company until "Big Bang" and financial deregulation in the City of London. The subsequent need for new skills caused it to change its policy and recruit extensively from outside.

Consultants such as CMG in the UK tend to recruit only experienced personnel because of the evident need for credibility with clients. In the case of GE-CGR it is a combination of growth and technological change calling for upgrading of personnel which has forced a change in policy.

"We search for two different types of people. We are hiring beginners, mainly engineers with a degree from a business school or an MBA; people with a double education so to speak. People coming out of schooling. And because our organisation is evolving, and because we are raising the overall level of competency of our people, sometimes for new positions, we don't have the talent yet within our company. So we need to look outside . . . although overall we prefer not to hire people from outside. We prefer to grow them ourselves."

Catching them young: the process of graduate recruitment

UK company practice

The UK has an enormous leeway to make up. The representation of graduates in management falls a long way short of the situation in the major competing nations at 20% compared with 60% in France and Germany and 85% in the USA.

This situation reflects a national culture affecting both the supply of graduates and the demand for them in industry. On the supply side there is a longstanding UK tradition of encouraging graduates to seek careers in the professions and the academic world rather than in industry and commerce. In recent years there have been vigorous attempts to change these attitudes, notably the campaign led by the Royal Society of Arts beginning with Industry Year in 1986. On the demand side many industries have only relatively recently systematically recruited graduates. Managers were in many cases recruited from the ranks of those who joined as school leavers and worked their way up, as in retail banking, for example. City jobs with higher status, as in merchant banking, were reserved for those privately and expensively educated at elite public schools. Technical experts acquired their qualifications by studying for the examinations of professional institutes by means of evening classes, sandwich courses or correspondence courses.

In the UK the market for graduates was reported on in 1990 by the Institute of Manpower Studies.[2] Demand for graduates has increased by 35% since 1980 and is expected to be at least 30% higher by 2000. Supply has grown by 12% from universities and 75% from polytechnics.[3] Universities account for 60% of all graduates. Apart from the special circumstances of recession in 1991–92 a substantial proportion of employers has reported recruitment difficulties in recent years, especially in technical and engineering disciplines. Growth in demand has been in excess of 150% (1979–88) in financial services, over 100% in other commerce, just under 100% in law, over 50% in accountancy but less than 20% in manufacturing and public services. Increased competition has led to revised recruitment strategies; less reliance on the January–March tour of the universities known as the "milk round", more use of recruitment fairs and increased expenditure on the design of recruitment literature. There is also a growing use of pre-recruitment programmes, such as providing work experience for "sandwich" students, forging links with particular academic departments, liaising with the schools and schools careers services and providing sponsorship for undergraduates. This practice now applies to one in three engineering students and is rapidly spreading to other sectors such as retailing and financial services. Another discernible trend is for blue-chip companies – exemplified in the present study by Kleinwort Benson, the BBC and Willis Corroon – to widen the net in the search for talent beyond Oxford and Cambridge and to take in people from other universities and polytechnics.

International recruiting, particularly with respect to continental Europe, is expected to grow rapidly during the 1990s. A survey of 153 graduate recruiters conducted by the journal *Graduate Post* in the autumn of 1990 asked which method respondents found most successful in attracting graduates. They were required to rank order eight possible approaches. The mean rank order given was as follows.

- The "milk round" (annual visits to the main university campuses).
- Recruitment brochures.
- Summer recruitment "fairs".
- Direct contacts with the departments or faculties of universities.
- Career directories.
- Advertising in newspapers or magazines.

- Sponsorship of students during their degree courses.
- Recruitment agencies.

The search for talent starts under all these headings, but a company's concern with the issue may be best revealed by the nature of the second item. Schofield[4] quotes, as an original approach to projecting a strong corporate image in the crowded financial services sector, the brochure put out by Bankers Trust, a merchant bank which places great emphasis on creativity and innovation and which is a major sponsor of the arts. This took the form of a fine art calendar on the theme "Originals". It featured paintings by young artists on the back of which were interviews with executives and recent young graduates presenting, indirectly, the bank's recruitment message.

Stoy Hayward is a medium-sized accountancy practice which sees itself as relatively unconventional and entrepreneurial. Operating in a market teeming with competitive firms vying with each other to recruit the best, Stoy Hayward took a high-risk approach by distributing a full-length paperback book entitled *Never Say Boring Again*. In it a young Stoy accountant has a range of adventures, surviving attempts at seduction, blackmail, bribery and assault.

Unilever is one of the world's largest manufacturers of fast-moving consumer goods. It is parent to hundreds of operating subsidiaries in many countries, employing graduates in various functions, and drawn from equally various disciplines. A traditional brochure describing all the relevant information about careers in Unilever would be dauntingly large, and the company has opted instead for a high-quality glossy magazine called *Managing Tomorrow*.

The two case histories which follow illustrate some of the best practice in British graduate recruitment.

CASE STUDIES

British Airways

British Airways claims to have the largest centralised commercial recruitment operation in the UK, run by a team of 90 full-time staff supported by a mainframe computer system. 3,000–5,000 people are recruited annually at all levels.

Some 72,000 applications are processed, of which 8,000 are from graduates; 13,000 interviews are held, 159,000 unsolicited enquiries are dealt with and 10,000 people walk in off the street seeking employment.

In 1989 the top management group in the human-resources function recognised some important trends, in particular that certain skills in fields such as information technology, finance and engineering were becoming more difficult to find, and that there was a downturn in the supply of young, talented people. At the same time business growth was generating rising demand. This realisation led to the setting up of a recruitment marketing team led by a recruitment marketing manager, Chris Wyche. The purpose of the new department was "to ensure consistency in the promotion of BA as a first-choice employer and to extend the company's customer-focused approach to the recruitment field".

Four operational recruitment teams were set up. Each of these, comprising about 18 people, focused on the needs of specific departments within the airline and made sure that a high level of service was provided to the line managers concerned.

The same basic customer service principles were applied to the recruitment operation and the airline's dealings with its passengers (many of the potential recruits were also, of course, actual or potential passengers).

There was a need to improve administration and communications which had suffered earlier in the 1980s when in conditions of economic recession there had always been a surplus of suitable applicants for jobs. Focusing on the two sets of "customers" for its services – external applicants and internal line managers – the department set out to measure the requirements for quality, quantity, timing and cost of the services to be provided for each. Guidelines were established for response targets in handling applications. In respect of graduates the target was that candidates should receive acknowledgement of an application within three days of its arrival at BA.

Four training programmes for line managers were developed.

- Addressing the demographic challenge.
- Recruitment skills within a global environment.
- Selection skills training.
- Effective recruitment for the 1990s.

The general economic climate and in particular the business conditions facing airlines have turned significantly less favourable since these initiatives were taken. Nevertheless BA recognises that the gap between the supply of talent and the demand for it will re-emerge with a vengeance when economic conditions improve and that only those companies which have maintained their commitment to communicating effectively with their potential employees will be able to meet their human-resource needs during the 1990s.

ICL

ICL is the UK's leading computer manufacturer, now Japanese owned.

Graduate recruitment is centralised. The company takes in the region of 300 graduates a year and processes about 5,000 applications. About half the 300 are sponsored engineering students destined for manufacturing, logistics and development. ICL accepts graduates from virtually any discipline for deployment in other functional areas such as sales, finance and personnel. It claims to have the highest offer/acceptance ratio in the UK computer industry and attributes this success to the care and consideration for candidates' needs and motives which are built into its procedures.

It was one of very few companies among those studied in the UK which had not cut back sharply on graduate intake as a result of the 1991–92 severe economic recession.

> "We learned from 1982 when we cancelled the graduate intake; it took us six years to recover from a poor image and we reaped the results. We have not stopped since. We have developed manpower planning models to determine the need, rather than how many we can afford."

ICL has taken part in the university milk round for the past five years or so and is represented at the major recruitment fairs, but places very considerable emphasis on sponsorship as a recruiting channel. 90% of sponsored students receive and accept job offers. It has a programme known as "Schools Connect" which links ICL senior managers with schools in their local communities. Given the key role of sponsorship in the company's strategy it is vitally important to target schools and a special brochure has been designed for this audience. There is also an ICL newspaper for students.

The company is one of the UK pioneers in the use of the assessment centre approach to initial selection. Candidates arrive in the afternoon in time to complete three pencil and paper tests before dinner. Over the meal they meet informally with the team of assessors and subsequently each gives a short presentation on a selected topic. The next day is spent carrying out a series of individual and group exercises and interviews. The pass rate at this stage, which is confined to shortlisted candidates, is 50%. ICL believes that as well as having superior predictive validity over other methods, the assessment centre carries important messages for candidates which aid the company's recruitment strategy. The method has high face validity, which means that all candidates, whether successful or not, tend to feel they have been fairly treated. Feedback is given to those who fail and in most cases is welcomed and seen as of value. The process gives time for candidates to explore issues of importance to them, such as the kind of bridge the company will provide between work and education. It enables them to get to know some key ICL people and to get a feeling for the company's relative informality.

ICL sees the whole recruitment process as a marketing exercise with the objective of getting the best people to apply to the company. It is among the leading UK based firms in moving into continental Europe in the search for talent. It aims to secure 10% of its UK recruits from European countries and claims to be one of the top ten European recruiters, building links with the universities, particularly in France, Germany, the Netherlands and Spain.

UK graduates' preferences

Among the UK companies taking part in the present study IBM (UK) was placed third in the "best of the best" list drawn up in 1990 of final year students' reactions to recruitment programmes[5] (Marks and Spencer came top). IBM's graduate recruitment brochure for 1990 also won first prize in a competition for the best graduate recruitment literature organised by the Industrial Society. It featured recent graduates already working for the company who were asked why they would recommend it. "I defy any firm to offer a better working environment with as much respect for the individual," said one, "and it's nice to work for a company that puts so much back into the community and the country in general."

One other company among those participating in the research for this book – Glaxo – featured in the UK top ten when the responses of MBAs were added to those of undergraduates.

A MORI survey of 1,015 final year undergraduates, also in 1990, listed 22 possible sources of information and asked which had been found most useful:

- in determining the type of career field the student would be interested in;

- for evaluating where there were jobs within the chosen career field; and
- in finding more detailed information on specific employers.

In response to this last question the most frequent response was recruitment brochures (26%), followed by literature written by their own careers office (14%). Talks with people working in the chosen field came close to this. In the same survey the undergraduates were asked what kind of information they were most interested in finding out when they first picked up an organisation's recruitment brochure. 47% wanted to know what the job would entail day to day; starting salary was some way behind this at 36%, closely followed by company location (34%). Training policy, career development and opportunities for promotion trailed behind.

Graduate recruitment: French and UK approaches compared

Graduate recruitment practices in French firms differ in several ways from those in the UK. There is no milk round. Instead French companies rely much more on direct applications from graduates plus networks of links with specific educational institutions. French companies tend to be more selective in terms of both the institutions and preferred subject disciplines. Graduates of the *grandes écoles* tend to be favoured over those from less vocationally oriented universities. French companies are more likely to employ staff exclusively for graduate recruitment purposes: about 75% compared with 39% in the UK.

Tony Keenan[6] reports the results of a survey of recruitment managers of 127 large UK organisations and 62 similar French firms. The average number of graduates recruited annually by the French companies was 100 compared with 75 for the UK companies. Nevertheless UK companies spent more on graduate recruitment.

Fewer than one in five UK companies were currently recruiting graduates from other EC countries, whereas 45% of the French organisations were doing so. 60% of the French recruiters had plans to increase this practice compared with only 40% of the British, so the gap is likely to widen.

Managers were given a list of potential graduate attributes and asked whether the importance of each would be likely to change following closer European economic integration. Most in both countries emphasised the growing importance of foreign language fluency. Four out of five of the French believe that future graduates should have more knowledge of European cultures, while fewer than half of the

British agreed.

Three-quarters of the French emphasised the need for work experience abroad but only a quarter of the British did so. 65% of the French thought it increasingly important that graduates should have received part of their education in another country but only one-fifth of the British held this view. Two-thirds of the French thought that willingness to work abroad would become more important compared with less than half of the British.

The case study of L'Oréal reinforces these findings.

CASE STUDY

L'Oréal

L'Oréal was founded in 1907 by a young chemical engineer, Eugene Schueller, a visionary who believed that the key to maintaining creativity, internationalism and sensitivity to customer needs was to seek the right sort of human talent. He saw the essence of the company not in its technology or material assets but in its people resources.

Expansion and diversification in recent years into other sectors such as publishing and television have created increasingly high demands for a broadly educated management body, with flexibility, top level technical expertise and, crucially, excellent interpersonal and communication skills.

In the interests of flexibility, L'Oréal has sought diversity in staff by recruiting from many different sources and many different disciplines. It is expanding recruitment beyond France as the global scale of business demands a wider mix of nationalities and cultures.

L'Oréal does not explicitly draw up criteria for recruitment. Nevertheless the most important criterion is willingness to work in a team. The recruiting process was described as "co-option". The decision is made with participation and input from all levels of the organisation so that it is based on consensus. The most important question is will he or she be able to live within the L'Oréal culture? This is described as "fervently anti-bureaucratic" and with a strong sense of "the way we do things around here", a process which relies heavily on an individual's personal skills rather than on laid down procedures to get things done.

Recruitment policies are not dictated from above nor are they written down. L'Oréal prefers to recruit "young cadres" and to shape and form them to integrate with the company culture, only exceptionally bringing in experienced people.

Recruiting practice in the USA

In the USA there is a strong tradition of close links between the business and academic worlds. This is manifest in the recruiting field. Given the huge number of institutions of higher education no company can hope to conduct a significant recruiting drive in them all, so it is normal practice to draw up a key list of up to 20–30 universities and to concentrate efforts on these. They will be chosen on the basis of reputation and standard of excellence in a particular field, the relevance of the curriculum to the activities of the business, experience with past recruiting in terms of retention rates and career progress, and also of geography. Given the size of the country there is much more regional recruiting by major companies than would be expected in European countries. There are clear regional labour markets even for the most highly qualified and it is sometimes difficult to persuade young graduates to be mobile and to relocate, for example, from North Carolina to Illinois.

The sheer scale of recruiting by the major US enterprises ensures that it is seen as a major business function and one calling for the involvement of senior line management. US practice is closer to German and French than to UK practice in the care taken to screen and recruit technically qualified graduates as distinct from liberal arts graduates. The five case studies which follow all illustrate this.

CASE STUDIES

Rockwell

Rockwell has one of the highest graduate acceptance ratios in the USA. The company attributes its success in recruiting to a number of factors, including the following.

- The visibility and prestige attached to the projects the company has been involved with: the Apollo space programme, space shuttles, B-1 strategic aircraft, "the things that engineers want to be involved in".
- The fact that the company can demonstrate that a very significant proportion of the top management were hired as college graduates and made successful careers within the business.
- Challenging initial assignments.
- First-class recruiting literature which really addresses the questions the students have.

Rockwell operates in a number of different technical fields — aerospace, avionics, automotive engineering, graphics and industrial automation — and is a leader in each. Recruiters representing these businesses visit most of the major engineering schools and interview 5,000–8,000 students each year. In addition large numbers of students at schools that are not visited mail applications either to corporate headquarters or to individual divisions. In a typical year Rockwell processes some 20,000 applications to fill 1,000 vacancies.

> "We are now in the process of looking at creative, innovative ways of early identification of some of those traits that we hold valuable so that we are not hiring just to fill an initial position, but hiring people that can potentially fill positions of greater and greater responsibility as time goes by."

The company also uses direct advertising. The brief to the agency was to produce something to seize the attention of the students. "One of the things about engineering students is that they don't have the time leisurely to read lots of extraneous material, so you've got to zero in." Rockwell also emphasised that since it was not interested in attracting the attention of liberal arts graduates, the advertisement should have something which would specifically appeal to the engineering mentality. To achieve this the advertisement featured the company's special award for outstanding technological achievement, the Leonardo da Vinci Medallion.

Rockwell recruits 30% of its engineer graduates from what it regards as the 30 top universities in this field: the ones with curricula that closely match the technology and projects the company is involved in. As well as the top national schools like MIT, Caltech and Stanford the list includes regionally recognised schools which can provide "hands-on" engineers who can get down to the detailed design, development and manufacturing tasks and ensure a good balance with the more analytical/theoretical approach of the majors.

Data General

Data General is an example of a smaller company trying to compete for the very best with giants like IBM, GE and Rockwell.

In normal times the company hires as many as 200 engineering graduates a year, but at the time of the study this had been cut back to 50 plus. The approach adopted was to establish a presence on a dozen or so campuses and really focus on 3–4. The aim was to confine recruiting to the very top schools and within this catchment area to those students with high accumulative grade averages. Success was achieved, in the face of strong competition, by "just getting out early, making contact early". Data General accepted that companies like Bell Labs, with considerable prestige in their favour, could also offer attractive assignments and had the financial muscle to offer very high starting salaries, but took the view that in the last analysis it was where the individual wanted to work that counted. One of Data General's attractions was that the vice-president of engineering was very well known in the industry, and people wanted to come and work for him. A widely read book about the company, *The Soul of a New Machine*, painted an accurate picture of an environment where people straight out of school could get significant responsibility and become involved in major projects. Students were attracted by the idea of an entrepreneurial atmosphere, a relatively small company and related chances to do things that might not be possible in larger concerns.

United Technologies

United Technologies focuses on 25 schools or universities for recruiting purposes, all ones with a strong technical curriculum, although some also have business curricula. The choice is determined by analysis of prior acceptance rates, geographic location, minimum acceptable entrance score on the Scholastic Aptitude Tests, the relevance of the curriculum to the company's activities and the value the school adds to the student. The company is also tracking past recruits, looking at retention and career progress in relation to university of origin.

Each university is allocated a top level executive whose primary responsibility is to build the relationship with that institution. At a less senior level a task force co-ordinator assists this executive in this work. The executive influences the awarding of grants by the company to the university. With some universities the company maintains relationships through its United Technology

Research Center. This is a facility dedicated to advanced research in the technologies of interest to the business and it has a long history of involving university research efforts in its work.

In times of economic surgence the company recruits around 700 graduates a year but in 1991 the number was reduced to 350 and in 1992 the target was 300.

Baxter Healthcare

Baxter emphasises the need to move from concentrating on senior undergraduates to undergraduates entering school. By developing relationships with these students earlier, Baxter has a broader base of experience from which to evaluate the skills of these candidates. The company is establishing goals whereby offers will be extended to students prior to their last year of university.

There are two primary programmes which support these goals. One, the "intern program", provides approximately 100–120 placements during the summer vacation with the aim of hiring those who make the grade. Another, the "co-op student program", involves giving the student a part-time job throughout his or her period of study. Baxter focuses its corporate efforts on 20 universities scattered across the country. Divisions can, however, recruit from other sources if so desired.

Baxter focuses its resources and efforts in becoming an active partner on campuses, identifying needs and then working collectively to support university objectives. Baxter has executives speak on campus or in class, builds relationships with professors, is involved with student organisations, and supports the efforts of Placement Centres by offering "mock interviews" or "how to interview" workshops, for example. While it does participate in providing grants and endowments to universities, this is typically not the most effective recruiting tool. Although universities welcome funding, activities such as those mentioned are becoming increasingly more valued by campuses and effective for companies. Baxter also participates in research, particularly with business schools or schools of organisational behaviour.

Recruiting of PhDs is done at the division level. It is believed to be a benefit to have one PhD discuss opportunities with another. Getting the company's top technical people out on the campuses and involved provides value in the recruiting process.

Recruiting of MBAs is also done at the division level and for specific functions.

During the 1970s there had been a corporate initiative to bring MBAs into the organisation, often in "assistant to" positions. Retention of these MBAs long-term, however, proved to be a challenge. In addition, existing long-term employees began to develop resentment and perceived that promotional opportunities were being given to the recently recruited MBAs rather than to current employees. Today, MBAs recruited at the divisions are assimilated into operating unit environments from the beginning of their careers.

Intel

A very high proportion of Intel's hiring is technical: electronics engineers, chemical engineers and physicists. There are a number of key universities designated as primary. The liaison with educational institutions starts at an earlier stage in the schools, seeking to influence the curriculum, especially in science and mathematics.

Intel is extremely well-known from a technical viewpoint, so the major task on campus is to make Intel equally well-known as a company. The starting point, however, is the clear advantage in recruiting technologists that goes with being a technical leader.

The company's approach is highly systematic and thoroughly planned. The objective, to be achieved by 1994/95, is to have 75% of all entry jobs filled by new college graduates (currently it is just over 65%). The long-term strategic hire programme is for 400–500 graduate entrants a year "almost whether we need them or not". The underlying purpose is to keep fresh ideas coming in.

SUMMARY

Companies seek out the best available talent for a variety of reasons, not simply for what they can do, or to provide a "bank" of talent against future needs. Other reasons include image-building and the attitude "only the best are good enough for us".

By contrast some companies do not reach out for the most talented, reflecting again a range of attitudes and motives. UK industry, in particular, has been slow to recruit graduates and, more recently, to recruit MBAs, reflecting an anti-intellectual, intensely practical tradition. Some companies emphasise team-building rather than recruiting highly talented individuals. Others prefer to search for and identify talent from within. Yet others react against the "prima donna" character-istics of some highly talented people.

Talent is recruited primarily at a young age and typically in the form of graduate entry. Search consultants and direct searches are used by companies mainly to fill a small number of key senior positions which become vacant or which arise because of changed technologies or changed market conditions.

Graduate recruitment in all the Western economies has become an intensively competitive activity. There are some interesting differences in approach from country to country. In the UK the chief instrument is the "milk round", a series of annual visits to the main campuses. The activity is in the main carried out by personnel staff. Recruitment brochures are considered the next most important tool, and student reactions confirm this.

The milk round does not exist in France where recruiters rely more upon links with selected educational institutions. French companies are more active in recruiting nationals from other countries than UK companies.

In the USA there is a strong tradition of links with the universities, but campus visiting is also widely practised. Compared with European companies US companies appear more likely to involve senior line managers in the recruitment process.

References

1 G.A. Randell, "Management Selection and Recruitment", in Bernard Taylor (ed.), *Management Development and Training Handbook*, Maidenhead, McGraw Hill, 1975.

2 Helen Connor, Marie Strebler and Wendy Hirsh, *You and Your Graduates: The First Few Years*, Brighton, Institute of Manpower Studies, Report No. 191, 1990.

3 In the UK the distinction between universities and polytechnics was abolished in 1992.

4 Philip Schofield, "The Difference a Graduate Brochure Can Make", *Personnel Management*, January 1991.

5 "Graduates Chosen Few", *Business*, September 1990.

6 Tony Keenan, "Graduate Recruitment à la Française", *Personnel Management*, December 1991.

5

SELECTING TALENT

The objectives of selection

Recruiting and selection are, of course, overlapping processes. The specification of the person required in a recruitment brief or advertisement is partially a selection process, in as far as it screens out (or seeks to screen out) potential applicants in terms of such attributes as educational attainment, experience or age. The development of a shortlist from applicants, all of whom to a greater or lesser degree meet the specification, is clearly and explicitly a selection process and often one involving extremely subjective judgments. The term "selection", however, is principally used for the final stage, which is the most difficult.

The objective of selection is ostensibly prediction. If there are ten vacancies and 30 candidates, the objective is to pick the ten most likely to meet the organisation's expectations in terms of performance. The British Broadcasting Corporation, in selecting for the core areas of talent, seeks to predict which of the applicants seeking entry to its training schemes is most likely – perhaps ten, perhaps 20 years on – to "make it" as, for example, editor of Panorama or producer of the series which knocks Independent Television's best "soap" off the top of the audience ratings. This example, the enormous difficulty of which is readily apparent, illustrates some of the issues involved in such selection.

The validity of selection

Selection procedures should meet three criteria.

- Do they actually measure what they claim to? (Construct validity)
- Do they measure it reliably? (Reliability)
- Do they predict job performance? (Predictive validity)

Predictiveness is usually expressed, in practice, as a correlation coefficient with 1.0 representing a perfect relationship between selection and subsequent performance and 0 indicating a relationship no greater than would be achieved by chance.

In order to establish validity four things are necessary.

1 A large number of applicants. Since a significant relationship between two variables can only be established on the basis of an adequate statistical sample, a large number of applicants is required. In many cases it takes several years before an adequate sample is built up and over such a period of time there will usually be changes in person specifications, reflecting changed job requirements, changes in the selection procedures themselves and changes in performance criteria. In the case of most companies the number of graduate entrants to trainee schemes in any one year is too small for a proper validation of selection and the accumulation of reliable data over time would tend to be jeopardised by some or all of the changes indicated above. In the case of selection of high flyers the numbers are of course much smaller.

2 A measurement scale for selection. It is necessary to have a measurement scale of some kind at the selection stage, perhaps on a scale of 1–10, so that different levels of performance can be related to different gradings achieved during the selection process. Since most selection procedures result merely in two discrete categories – those who pass and those who fail – this condition is not met.

3 Measurement of subsequent performance. There is need for an equally finely graded measurement of each applicant's subsequent performance. This can be achieved through a performance appraisal procedure designed for this purpose, but most performance appraisal schemes have other objectives such as setting performance standards or identifying training needs. In addition, most performance appraisals are highly subjective.

4 Selection and performance criteria. This is where a real test of validity becomes virtually impossible to achieve in practice since selection and performance criteria are needed in respect of all applicants, not just those deemed to have passed by the selectors. In fact, of course, few if any of those rejected by a company are followed up so there is no way of knowing whether or not they were validly rejected.

In most cases of selection procedures for highly talented people there is no systematic and rigorous approach to establishing the validity of the procedure and no way, therefore, of demonstrating that money spent on improving selection procedures has been wisely invested.

There are, however, some grounds other than pure faith for believing that the efforts are justified.

- There is abundant evidence from studies of selection procedures in instances involving quite specific measurable criteria and large numbers of cases that expenditure on improving selection procedures is more than justified financially, in terms of improved performance and reduced turnover. One example is the selection of pilots for the Royal Air Force or for the US Air Force.
- By using a technique called meta-analysis, Hunter and Hunter in the USA[1] have combined the results of many small studies to produce findings based on large numbers. Although their findings should be treated with caution, they indicate the achievement of validity coefficients of the following levels for various selection methods.

Assessment centres	0.42–0.64
Personality tests	0.41 (combined average)
Biodata	0.38
Structured interviews	0.32
Unstructured interviews	0.15
References	0.12
Graphology	0

Specifying requirements

Selection procedures, at least in theory, are concerned with matching applicants to jobs. It follows that there should be a clear view as to the nature of the job to be carried out and of the knowledge, skills and other qualities required if it is to be carried out effectively. There is, in other words, a requirement for a job specification (what is to be done) and a person specification (the ideal attributes of the person engaged to do it).

This theory works well with respect to jobs involving less complex, less intangible patterns of human behaviour than those with which this book is concerned. For example, the knowledge, skills and other qualities required of a heavy goods truck driver can be relatively easily specified following a step-by-step analysis of the activities of skilled drivers. In the case of an investment analyst, an expert in twelfth century English silver, a creative software writer, a marketing manager or a programme maker for the BBC, however, the task is much more difficult.

Companies tend at this point to fall into two categories. On the one hand there are those which attempt systematically, and in some considerable detail, to analyse jobs and come up with person specifications. Such approaches sometimes involve using standard analytical tools like the Professional and Managerial Position Questionnaire or the Occupational Analysis Inventory in the USA or the Work Profiling System developed by Saville and Holdsworth in the UK. Most companies take the view that managerial work lends itself to this approach and it has been analysed in terms of specific competencies by Boyatzis[2] in the USA and on a national scale by the Management Charter Initiative in the UK.

A technique known as Repertory Grid Analysis has been used to identify key skill requirements in the case of top level UK civil servants. The starting point is to draw up a list of tasks. These are then grouped in threes and people familiar with the tasks are asked to say which is the odd one out in terms of skill requirements and why. This results in a list of skills. Each task is then graded in terms of how much of each of the skills is involved in its execution. Thus the civil servants started with a list of 26 frequently occurring tasks, including motivating staff, allocating priorities, producing written reports and supporting ministers when giving evidence to Select Committees of the House of Commons or the House of Lords. The tasks finally identified as demanding the highest levels of skill (Smith and others[3]) were as follows.

- Oral presentations and briefings to ministers.
- Appearing before Select Committees or the Public Accounts Committee.
- Planning the implementation of policies.
- Supporting ministers or heads of departments at Select Committee hearings.

This is, in effect, the job specification. The skills required – in other words the person specification – include the following.

- Analytical ability.
- Oral presentation skills.

- Management skills.
- Detailed specialist knowledge.
- Drafting skills.
- Decision-making skills.
- Breadth of outlook.

The question left unanswered, perhaps because it is unanswerable, is how, with any confidence, can young people be selected for civil service careers at the age of 21 with such potential that they will be competent to brief ministers some 15–20 years later?

The BBC exemplifies the alternative approach, one common in cases in which the task is seen as being highly creative. There is no attempt to conduct a rigorous, systematic analysis of the tasks – in this case those of news editor, producer, director, presenter, and so on – on the reasonable grounds that the process would be doomed to fail as the tasks are unanalysable. In consequence the person specification is derived in other, inevitably more subjective ways and is expressed in more general terms such as intellect, creativity and energy.

In the case of L'Oréal, too, there is no attempt to draw up explicit criteria for selection. The company looks for "strong personal qualities and skills". The most important criterion is that new recruits must be willing to work in a team. The most important question to be asked before an applicant is accepted is: "Will he or she be able to live within the L'Oréal culture?"

Alternative selection objectives

This last point raises the issue of the objectives of the selection process, which can all too easily be taken for granted. As well as trying to select people who will do the job superbly well (whatever the job may be) there may well be other objectives in the case of outstanding talent, some of which may not be made explicit.

One objective, as in the L'Oréal case, may be to identify people who will fit in with the existing company culture. Several of the companies in the present study acknowledged this as an explicit objective of their selection procedure. Another is to achieve some particular balance among the employed group, perhaps in terms of sex, socioeconomic background or ethnic origin. Some organisations were deliberately seeking diversity among the intake in the interest of creativity; others were responding to actual or potential political pressures.

Selection methods

The main selection methods in use in respect of high-talent personnel are assessment centres, personality tests, interviews, biodata and graphology. Each approach will be briefly reviewed in terms of what is involved and issues of validity.

Assessment centres

Assessment centres developed out of various selection procedures in use in military organisations, including pre-war German attempts to identify leadership potential, UK army War Office selection boards and the assessment procedures developed by the US Office of Strategic Services. The classical model which has most influenced practice in recent years was first developed within AT&T in the 1950s.

At the third International Congress on the Assessment Centre method, Quebec 1975, the conference endorsed the recommendations of a task force which proposed the following seven conditions which needed to be met for recognition of an assessment process as a valid assessment centre.

- Multiple assessment techniques must be used.
- Multiple assessors must be involved and they must have received training.
- Judgments and outcomes must be based on pooled information from both the techniques and the assessors.
- An overall assessment of behaviour must be made by the assessors at a separate time from the observation of behaviour.
- Simulation exercises must be used.
- The attributes or qualities to be assessed must be determined by an analysis of job requirements.
- The techniques used should be designed to provide information for the evaluation of these attributes or qualities.

Centres have been frequently used to identify long-range potential for top jobs and follow-up research indicates that they do predict the managerial level which participants will reach many years later. Such validation studies have been carried out, for example, in AT&T and the UK Civil Service. The validity may, however, reflect a self-fulfilling prophecy, since those successful at the assessment stage usually gain access to programmes of accelerated management development. Nevertheless research shows that assessment centre ratings are better predictors than personality tests, clinical judgments, interviews or supervisors' ratings. In particular they have been shown to outperform most other selection methods in predicting managerial success.

Much depends, of course, on the nature and appropriateness of the validation criteria used. Managerial success can be measured in a number of ways, including job performance (the most relevant but also the most difficult to define and measure), managerial level achieved, salary achieved and training success. Ideally multiple criteria should be used. A danger to be aware of is that the assessors, usually line managers, are influenced by their knowledge of the type of person who, traditionally, has moved into top jobs in the organisation and give higher ratings to those who fit the pattern and conform to the expectations of the corporate culture.

Assessment centres are also used to identify training and development needs. The use of centres for this purpose is growing but so far there has been less research into their effectiveness.

Participants in assessment centres, whether used for selection, identification of potential or identification of development needs, generally take a positive view of them and regard them as a more accurate, fair and valid technique than other methods.

A thorough and systematic job analysis is usually considered as a vital component in the design of an assessment centre. There is some difference between UK and US practice here. Americans tend to use a combination of standardised checklists and questionnaires, interviews and the "critical incidents" technique. The latter involves asking managers to think of non-routine occurrences where successful performance was critical for job success and to identify precisely both what they did and what skills or qualities enabled them to act effectively.

This technique is not uncommon in UK centres, but more extensive use is made of the "repertory grid" technique referred to previously. Managers are asked to think of a number of effective and ineffective managers known to them personally. Systematic comparisons between these managers results in the identification of a number of constructs that are perceived as discriminating between them and these are used in establishing the criteria employed.[4]

The job analysis results in descriptions of the desired skills, qualities or competencies associated with success. Usually up to 12 competencies are identified. Ideally these should be precisely defined, related to observable behaviour and presented in scalar form.

The exercises used include in-basket exercises, leaderless group discussions, case studies, various pencil and paper tests, questionnaires, role plays and interviews. In most cases the assessors are line managers drawn from the organisation. They bring with them knowledge of the job and of its organisational context, but they need training in the use and interpretation of tests and behavioural exercises. Their involvement is essential if they are to feel "ownership" of the results and motivated to act on them.

Among the companies in the present sample National Westminster Bank uses a full assessment centre procedure at the initial selection stage.

Personality testing

The word "personality" is used to refer to a set of relatively stable attributes or "traits" which an individual possesses and which, taken together, result in the characteristic ways of behaving which distinguish one from another. The behaviour is observed and related to such traits as introverted, excitable, moody, warm, idealistic, assertive, etc.

In theory there are some personality types which are more likely than others to be successful in particular social roles, particularly ones which involve intensive interaction with others. It is also believed that certain personality types will make a better fit with a given corporate culture than others.

This, then, is the rationale for attempting to assess personality as part of the selection process. The question of how to do it is highly controversial. Some prefer the systematic observation of behaviour in groups; others believe the exploration of personality in the interview is the best approach; in France it is widely accepted that the best clue to personality is handwriting; some selectors even use astrology. There is growing acceptance and use of pencil and paper tests, however, and there is now a very large number of such instruments available on the market.

There has been sharp criticism of personality tests. Blinkhorn and Johnson[5] examined a large number of validation studies and found that the majority were statistically flawed; they concluded that there were no grounds for supposing that personality tests predict performance at work to any useful extent, except in the case of somewhat extreme situations such as having to endure severe social isolation.

The defenders of the use of the tests deploy a number of arguments in their favour. In *Personnel Management*, September 1991, six British chartered psychologists gave their views, as follows.

- The statistical technique known as meta-analysis, developed over the past ten years, has made it possible to combine the results of a number of studies and thus to build a sufficiently large sample to justify rigorous statistical analysis. Studies focusing on personality testing have found tests to have validity on some dimensions. For example, a measure of conscientiousness was found to be consistently related to job performance while a measure of extraversion was a valid predictor of success in managerial and sales jobs.

- Although validity coefficients are not large (0.26 at most) relative to coefficients obtained for intelligence tests, they are significant enough to be useful. (A correlation of 0.20 produces a 20% better than chance outcome of the selection procedure.)

- Relatively few procedures involve the use of personality tests in isolation. They are used as one element in a complex pattern of information about an individual.

- Tests are most useful when interpreted by qualified and experienced psychologists who understand the supporting theories of personality upon which they are based.

- The apparent validity of the tests may be lowered by the fact that performance data are unavailable for those who take the test but are subsequently rejected by the selection process.

The tests fall into two broad categories according to the underlying theory of personality on which they are based. One approach is to conceptualise personality types following the theories of Carl Jung. The most well-known and widely used test of this kind is the Myers Briggs Type Indicator. The alternative approach is based on the conceptualisation of personality in terms of combinations of discrete traits. The most well-known and widely used test of this kind is Cattell's 16 PF (Personality Factors) Test.

The selection interview

"Employment interviewing is like sex and driving; most people rate themselves highly, the consequences of mistakes can be serious, when something goes wrong there is a tendency to blame the other party and nonetheless most of us continue to do it."[6]

The 16 PF Test

Cattell's 16 factors are as follows.

1	Reserved, detached, critical, aloof	Outgoing, warm-hearted, easy-going, participating
2	Less intelligent, concrete thinking	More intelligent, abstract thinking
3	Affected by feelings, emotionally less stable, easily upset	Emotionally stable, faces reality, calm nature
4	Humble, mild, accommodating and conforming	Assertive, aggressive, stubborn, competitive
5	Sober, prudent, serious, taciturn	Happy-go-lucky, impulsive, lively, enthusiastic
6	Expedient, disregards rules, feels few obligations	Conscientious, persevering, staid, masochistic
7	Shy, restrained, timid	Venturesome, socially loved, uninhibited, spontaneous
8	Tough-minded, self-reliant, realistic, no-nonsense	Tender-minded, clinging, overprotected, sensitive
9	Trusting, adaptable, free of feeling, easy to get along with	Suspicious, self-opinionated, hard to fool
10	Practical, careful, conventional	Imaginative, careless of practical matters, Bohemian
11	Forthright, artless, natural, unpretentious	Shrewd, calculating, worldly
12	Self-assured, confident, serene	Apprehensive, self-reproaching, worrying, troubled
13	Conservative, respecting established ideas	Experimenting, liberal, free-thinking, radical
14	Group dependent, a "joiner" and sound follower	Self-sufficient, prefers own decisions, resourceful
15	Undisciplined self-conflict, follows own urges, careless of protocol	Controlled, socially precise, following self-image
16	Relaxed, languid, unfrustrated	Tense, frustrated, driven, overwrought

Recent surveys have shown that in the UK the use of personality tests has doubled in two years, with 58% of employers now using some psychometric tests. Three-quarters of university students complete a form of psychometric test. Research in 1991 by Kerr Brown Associates[7] showed that 74% of job applicants had taken an aptitude test and 47% a personality test. Only half were given any feedback and only 2.8% thought that tests allowed them to present themselves favourably, compared with 72% who chose the interview.

Few companies involved in this research were using psychometric tests of personality, but notable exceptions were British Airways and National Westminster Bank. One US company used personality tests in the past but no longer does so. The reasons were partly to do with cost and partly because many applicants resented them. It was felt that there might be some very highly talented people who, on principle, would not wish to take the tests and would thus be lost.

The Myers Briggs Type Indicator

The MBTI was developed by two American psychologists, Katherine Briggs and Isabel Myers. It provides a measure or indicator of personality by looking at eight behavioural preferences organised into four scales. The preferences from each scale are combined to indicate the respondent's particular type.

The test is well researched and documented over a 40 year period. Nevertheless its results should always be treated carefully and challenged.

The four scales are as follows.

1 Extraversion or introversion (E or J). This scale refers to how a person is energised. Extroverts prefer to draw their energy from the outside world of people, activities or things while introverts prefer to draw their energy from their internal world of ideas, emotions or impressions.

2 Sensing or intuition (S or N). This refers to how people prefer to attend to things or take in information. Sensing involves a preference for concrete reality and accepting information through the five senses; being intuitive is to rely more on the sixth sense, to imagine what might be rather than concentrate on what is.

3 Thinking or feeling (T or F). This refers to the decision-making process. Thinking involves deciding things in a logical, rational way whereas feeling involves deciding things in a personal way based on values and feelings.

4 Judgment or perception (J or P). A preference for judgment is a preference for living life in a planned and organised way and the converse – perception – is a preference for living a spontaneous and flexible life.

Combining the four scales gives 16 possible types.

The four groups
The 16 types have been grouped into four categories in respect of their approach to leadership.

1 The stabiliser group. This consists of ESTJ, ISFJ, ISTJ, ESFJ. As managers, they stabilise, establish and maintain the rules and procedures. They conduct affairs in an orderly way, run efficient meetings, cope well with detail.

2 The visionary group. This embraces the types ENTJ, INTJ, ENTP, INTP. These are the ones who come up with the ideas, who devise models and systems, question the status quo, focus on possibilities, pioneer fresh approaches.

3 The negotiators. These are ESTP, ESFP, ISFP and ISTP. They are the "fire-fighters", the ones who cope with crisis, who deal with problems expeditiously, who live very much in the present.

4 The catalysts. These are ENFJ, INFJ, INFP and ENFP. Their strength lies in drawing the best out of others, giving and receiving feedback, speaking and making presentations, communicating, caring and enthusiasm.

Organisations need all types.

- Stabilisers to lend stability and confidence.
- Visionaries to provide visions and models for change.
- Negotiators to solve problems and lend excitement.
- Catalysts to "lubricate the interpersonal fabric".

In the USA Michael Lyons[8] used the Myers Briggs Type Indicator with 1,000 IT professionals to establish the "Data Processing Psyche". The most common type found was ISTJ. The main differences between DP managers and general managers were that the latter were twice as likely to be extroverted and tended to show a higher preference for feeling and judging.

A sample of 1,000 managers drawn from a wide range of functions attending programmes at Ashridge Management College showed that ISTJ types constituted the largest single group at 19% of the total. In the USA and Japan, however, managers are predominantly ENTJ.

Common factors between the two groups included liking to create, design and build and being people-oriented, effective at building alliances and coalitions and having good communication skills.

The author of this remark identifies three main types of approach:

- the biographical, almost certainly the most common;
- the problem-solving, in which the candidate is given a hypothetical problem to discuss; and
- the stress interview, in which the interviewer uses an aggressive approach in order to place the candidate under pressure.

Interviews, one-to-one or by a panel, single or several, are far and away the most widely used selection method. Interviewing is by its nature a highly subjective process and validation studies show that its predictive validity is low. It is, however, backed up by a long tradition of acceptance and it has a certain "face validity". It is an acceptable, non-threatening, "safe" process for interviewer and candidate alike. It was certainly the most favoured selection method among the companies which supplied information in the current research.

It goes without saying that interviewers should be trained in the art but the more senior they are the less likely this will be the case. Validation studies also show that structured and carefully prepared interviews are more likely to have predictive validity than unstructured ones. Again, however, the more senior the person or persons conducting the interview the more likely it is that the questioning will be unstructured.

There are many guides to sound interviewing practice and this is not the place to reiterate the recommended procedures to be followed in the standard interview. There are some things that can usefully be said, however, about the special factors which apply in the case of highly talented personnel.

If they are being recruited direct from university or college and have no significant employment track record the main task of the interviewer is to try to uncover evidence of exceptional ability. The standard approach is to focus on two things – academic attainment and achievement in extra-curricular activities – particularly where these give evidence of leadership at an early age. These should, of course, be identified, but deeper probing may well uncover other important facts. These may involve unusual hobbies, resilience in the face of severe trauma or deprivation, actions which illustrate unusual levels of self-reliance and the like. Research into the biographical details of outstanding achievers shows a reasonably common pattern of such things and if they are brought to light the range of information available to the selectors is greatly enriched.

In the case of the mature, experienced candidate, assuming that the search and shortlisting processes have been carried out thoroughly and efficiently, the interview has only one objective, which is to establish whether or not the candidate will fit into the corporate culture. Referring to direct entrants to senior posts the spokesperson of one major company said: "They don't stay long. It's as if we have an immune system which expels antibodies. Perhaps this is because of our distinctive culture. It is unforgiving and immensely political."

Keith Bedell-Pearce, chief executive of Prudential Financial Services, when preparing for this type of interview writes down "what I feel are the job requirements, what I feel are the qualities required, including the chemistry of the relationship between the candidate and myself".

Biodata

There has been considerable interest, mainly in the USA, in attempting to apply rigorous tests of validity to biographical data. In practice, however, a 1983 survey[9] showed that of 437 US firms responding only 11% were using the weighted scoring system for application forms which represents the systematic use of biodata. The biodata approach to selection is based on assumptions about the interaction of personal qualities and life experience: on the one hand the ways in which particular characteristics are developed through particular kinds of experience; and on the other the influence of an individual's personal qualities in determining the kinds of experience he or she acquires.

Biodata are usually collected on forms which use a multiple choice format to facilitate subsequent scoring. The questions are partly factual, for example, the number of siblings, or position in family, and partly to do with attitudes, values or preferences. The candidate's answers are combined to produce a score which is then used as a selection filter.

The construction of the biodata questionnaire involves several stages. First, as with other selection techniques, the skills and competencies believed to relate to successful job performance are identified. Second, a range of experiential and attitudinal items is generated, perhaps using a "brainstorming" approach, which seem likely to relate to the skills or competencies. For example, if creativity is a required characteristic an experimental question might ask the following.

Have you ever:

(a) Painted a picture?

(b) Written a poem?
(c) Written a story?
(d) Invented something useful?
(e) Designed your ideal house?

The resulting questionnaire is then given to as large a sample as possible of existing employees for whom success criteria are available. The responses of this sample should then be subject to statistical analysis to identify those items with the strongest relationships with success.

The questionnaire is then reformulated to exclude items with little or no predictive validity and used in practice.

Several validation studies of biodata have been carried out and most have found that the technique is one of the best tools available to selectors. Face validity is a problem, however; few candidates would relish the thought that they had been rejected because they were the youngest of three siblings.

Graphology

This technique is very little used in the UK or USA but is in quite common usage in continental Europe. Chartered psychologists in the UK virtually unanimously unceremoniously dismiss the approach as worthless, yet it is standard procedure in many French companies. It was in use in GEC-ALSTHOM, for example.

Rigorous validation studies are rare and those that do appear in academic journals are mainly in German and French and have remained untranslated into English.

A common criticism is that the personality profiles produced by graphologists are so general in nature that they could apply to almost anyone. Fowler,[10] however, quotes examples of personality descriptions which do distinguish clearly between individuals. There is no argument about the observable fact that people display highly individual handwriting characteristics, nor about the fact that those characteristics are stable over time.

Graphological analysis can be validated in three ways.

• Comparisons between the results of graphology and those of well-validated conventional psychometric tests. Fowler quotes several studies which attempted such comparisons. In some other cases there were significant but weak correlations, in others there were no statistically significant correlations.

- Descriptive validity. This is the ability to produce a narrative style picture of a personality such that people who know the subject well can readily single it out from a range of descriptions of some other subjects. Fowler quotes two studies of the validity of graphology in this sense, both of which found statistically significant results.
- Predictive validity. Such studies are more important but produce very conflicting results. In one study quoted by Fowler validity coefficients as high as 0.85 were found in the context of managerial work. Yet in another study involving sales personnel no significant relationship was found.

Fowler, who is a practising personnel manager rather than an academic psychologist, concluded from his study of the subject that there is something in graphology which merits more serious attention than it has been given in the UK and USA in the past. Although the use of graphology by itself as a predictive device cannot, in his view, be recommended, there is enough evidence to justify further research. He makes the final point that it is a technique which could be used without a candidate's prior knowledge and agreement and points to the large percentage of job advertisements in continental European publications which call for the candidate's CV to be accompanied by a handwritten letter without specifying the use to which the letter will be put.

UK and French selection methods compared

The use of graphology apart, there are marked differences between UK and French companies over the selection of potential managers. A study of 73 UK and 52 French organisations made in 1989[11] found that they were closest in the use of interviews (always used by 94% of French companies and 90% of UK companies). However, more than one interview was used by 97% of French companies but only 60% of UK companies, and French companies were more likely to involve line managers in the interviewing (87% always did so compared with 78%). The French interviews were more likely to be one-on-one.

French companies made more use of application forms (89% compared with 70% always used), personality tests (17% compared with 10%) and handwriting analysis (17% compared with nil). UK companies made more use of references (74% compared with 11%), cognitive tests (12% compared with 7.5%), biodata (4% compared with nil) and assessment centres (4% compared with nil).

SUMMARY

Validating the selection methods used to select highly talented recruits to industry is extremely difficult and is rarely systematically carried out. Research, however, gives grounds for believing that investing in improved selection methods pays off. Among orthodox methods, assessment centres, personality tests and biodata questionnaires have relatively high predictive validity, while references and unstructured interviews are little better than chance.

An important first step is to attempt to specify as precisely as possible the qualities and attributes being looked for. This is easier with respect to the more straightforward managerial tasks than with respect to work which is highly creative. In some cases the objective of selection has less to do with predicting job performance and is more concerned with assessing the extent to which individuals will fit the corporate culture.

Assessment centres are widely used in UK and US companies. Arguments in their favour include not only evidence as to their validity but also the fact that they produce generally favourable reactions in candidates. They are, however, costly to run.

Personality tests are also widely used. Opinion among psychologists is sharply divided on the question of their usefulness and they often provoke negative reactions among candidates.

The interview remains the main selection method for many companies, among them the largest and most sophisticated, despite doubts about its validity.

Biodata methods – using biographical questionnaires – are not yet in widespread use despite encouraging information about their validity.

Many French companies and some in other European countries use graphology but this method attracts little support and has low credibility in the UK or USA.

References

1 J.E. and R. Hunter, "Validity and Utility of Alternate Predictions of Job Performance", *Psychological Bulletin*, vol. 96, pp. 72–88, 1984.
2 R.E. Boyatzis, *The Competent Manager: A Model for Effective Performance*, New York, John Wiley, 1982.
3 Mike Smith, Mike Gregg and Dick Andrews, *Selection and Assessment: A New Appraisal*, London, Pitman, 1989.
4 Margaret Blanksby and Paul Iles, "Recent Development in Assessment Centre Theory, Practice and Operation", *Personnel Review*, vol. 19, no. 6, pp. 33–43, 1991.
5 Steve Blinkhorn and Charles Johnson, "Personality Tests: the Great Debate", *Personnel Management*, September 1991.
6 T. Watson, "Recruitment and Selection" in K. Sissons (ed.), *Personnel Management in Britain*, Oxford, Basil Blackwell, 1989.
7 *Personnel Management*, February 1992.
8 Michael Lyons, "The DP Psyche", *Datamation*, August 1985.
9 R.L. Mathis and J.H. Jackson, *Personnel*, St Paul Min, West, 1985.
10 Alan Fowler, "An Even-handed Approach to Graphology", *Personnel Management*, March 1991.
11 Viv Shackleton and Sue Newell, "Management Selection: A comparative survey of methods used in top British and French companies", *Journal of Occupational Psychology*, vol. 64, Part 1, pp. 23–36, 1991.

6

MANAGING TALENT FOR PERFORMANCE

The higher the level of talent, the greater the challenge to companies to find more effective ways of managing it for productivity and performance.

The central problem is of course how to create conditions which simultaneously provide for above average commercial performance and the fullest possible expression of the talents of individual employees. Making gifted people productive for their organisations is not, in most instances, a matter of getting them to work harder or smarter. They are usually so involved in their work and so bright that such interventions are irrelevant. The managerial task is much more to do with dismantling barriers to performance and productivity and channelling efforts into avenues which will directly contribute to the achievement of the organisation's goals.

The process of influence

Thus performance management in the case of highly talented people is best looked upon as a process of influence. The outcome should be for them to understand and identify with the organisation's objectives and see how their own contribution can be enhanced.

In exercising this process managers must take full account of the preferred ways of working of talented people. Current assumptions about productivity are based on nearly a century of experience of managing for productivity following the pioneering work of Frederick Taylor.[1] These ideas are based on the notion of "labour productivity", that is, the measured (and measurable) outputs of work achieved from the application of measured (and measurable) inputs of labour. Outputs are measured in terms of standard products and inputs in terms of man-hours or man-days on the assumption that an hour's labour by one worker is much the same as an hour's labour by another and in any case, unless the workers are on piece rates, represents a standard unit of cost.

The higher the level of talent of the individual, and the more complex the task, the less likely is it that either outputs or inputs can be so readily quantified.

A research scientist in a pharmaceutical company, for example, may follow a particular set of ideas through over many months, working excessive hours, only to conclude that that particular approach leads nowhere. How is the value of such a negative output to be assessed? Has the time of the scientist concerned been used effectively? It is certainly possible to arrive at a calculation of the cost to the company of the time spent on the project, but by what standards of judgment can it be decided whether or not the time was utilised efficiently? If it took six months to reach the conclusion that that particular line of research should not be pursued further could another researcher have reached the same conclusion in three months? Or might it have taken someone less talented twice as long? Or, even more to the point, might a more talented researcher have discovered that it was, after all, a viable route to a new product? There is also the possibility – and there are many examples of this, including the famous 3M Post-it – that in the course of the project, through serendipity, an altogether different product from the one being sought might have been discovered and proved to be a winner.

One respondent summed up this issue as follows:

> "That's one of the difficulties, that a person spends two years working on something and it doesn't end up in a product for the company. Other decisions come into why it isn't used and maybe five years down the road they reach back, take that development and use it after all."

This is not to argue that any attempt to influence the performance of highly talented employees should be abandoned as a hopeless task, but rather that it should be thought through afresh. Conventional thinking and practice in the field of productivity management has to be cleared away.

The starting point in the process should be the development of a very clear understanding of the various influences which, taken together, will determine how well a talented person performs.

A model of these influences is shown in Figure 1.

The contribution of the individual

As the figure suggests, an individual has an option to develop their

Figure I **Factors affecting the performance of talented people**

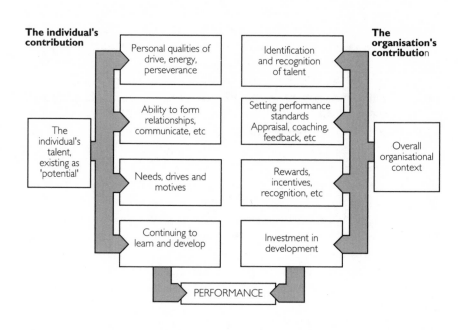

own talent, which is a potential waiting to be harnessed via appropriate assignments. (To quote Drucker[2] again, talent is like electricity: of no use unless it is being put to work.) This talent is relative; the more scarce it is, the greater its potential value and the stronger its capacity to confer competitive advantage on the organisation which uses it wisely.

The personal qualities of the individual will affect his or her ability to harness talent effectively and sustain a high level of performance. Under this heading fall such attributes as energy, stamina, determination, perseverance, self-confidence, emotional stability, flexibility and tolerance of stress. The ability to communicate is crucial, in combination with empathy and extraversion, in determining how well the individual will fit into a team or be capable of building productive relationships with other people.

Needs, drives and motivation will determine how the individual responds to those aspects of organisational life which, whether designed for the purpose or not, have a significant impact on energy and enthusiasm.

Self-development is the final and perhaps most crucial factor. The most valuable talent will accept responsibility for the process of continuous learning which is needed to stay at peak level.

The contribution of the organisation

The organisation must, initially, establish an overall framework in terms of structure, culture and style of management which offers an ambience in which talent can flourish.

In *The 100 Best Companies to Work For in America*[3] the authors describe a number of talent-intensive companies which have set out to achieve such an ambience and have, in the opinion of the authors, largely succeeded. The companies which are given the maximum score on a five-point scale used to assess "ambience" are Apple Computer, Bell Laboratories, Hewlett Packard, Kollmargen Corporation and Odetics Inc. Among the companies contributing to the present study, a score of four out of five was achieved by Baxter Healthcare, IBM, Merck and J.P. Morgan. How some of these and some European companies create such an ambience will be discussed in Chapter 8.

Within such a framework the specific actions called for are as follows.

- The identification and recognition of outstanding talent wherever it is to be found. It is increasingly recognised that both for reasons of equity and to deal with severe shortages of certain kinds of talent, companies must widen the search for talent beyond the traditional institutional sources – Oxbridge, the *grandes écoles*, the Ivy League – and beyond the traditional white, male-dominant group. They must discover the talent emerging from regional or specialist colleges, talented women, talented Asians and blacks and talent already in the business but trapped at shop-floor level.

  Xerox is an excellent example of this approach. It set out to achieve at all levels a "balanced workforce" some years ago and built up both its expertise in selection and assessment and its reputation for equality of opportunity.

  > "Our job of recruiting and finding high potential black talent, for example, has been made much easier by the work we did 20 years ago. ... We have chosen as a mission that by the year 2000 we would like to be seen as 'the employer of choice' for women scientists."

- Setting, in partnership with the individuals concerned, clear task objectives and performance standards.

- The provision of a range of supportive and developmental processes designed both to monitor performance and to provide paths to its improvement. These include appraisal, counselling, coaching, mentoring and feedback in various forms.
- The provision of a range of incentives, rewards and reinforcement processes designed to meet the motivational patterns of the types of talented people concerned.
- Investing in the maintenance and further development of talent. Such investment involves not only the financial outlay involved in providing for places on formal training courses. Of greater significance still is the investment in the form of top management time and commitment.

What companies are doing to create the appropriate organisational framework for the management of talent will be examined in Chapter 8. The nature of talented peoples' motives and the ways in which organisations approach motivation will be treated in Chapter 7, and the processes of development, particularly in respect of high flyers, in Chapter 9. The remainder of this chapter will be devoted to the issues of objective setting and performance standards, together with those processes such as appraisal, coaching and mentoring which are closely associated with the management of performance.

The objectives of talented people's work

The management of the performance of talented people needs as its basis a clear understanding of the nature of the desired outputs of their work. This understanding needs to be mutual, and it certainly cannot be taken for granted that it exists naturally. Bringing it about will often take a good deal of discussion and a willingness to see the other's point of view on the part of both parties.

Graphic designers working in an agency focusing on developing corporate and brand images tend to define desirable outputs of their work in such terms as winning design awards, meeting with approval among their peers in the industry, and providing them with pieces which when incorporated into a portfolio of work will significantly enhance their personal market value in the design field. Agency managers, on the other hand, place priority on work which keeps the client happy, which is produced on time and within budget. These differing ideas about objectives need reconciling if the organisation is to survive, both in the short term by virtue of its ability to keep its clients and serve them profitably, and over the long term by virtue of its ability to attract, retain and motivate the best talent among young designers leaving college.

A second factor to be taken into consideration is the ill-defined or indefinable nature of the output of much of the work carried out by very talented people. In the case of most of the tasks which society requires the most talented of the population to attend to, the work is unanalysable and unprogrammable in the sense that neither the end-product nor the steps taken to produce it can be precisely described in advance. A poem, a symphony or a piece of sculpture fall obviously into this category. Less obviously, so does the development of a strategic vision for a business, the carrying out of a counselling interview, the development of a new software package or the assembly of an investment portfolio.

With hindsight, of course, it is possible to recognise a successful strategy, a counselling interview which resulted in a transformation of attitude and performance, a software package that works, or the investment portfolio which beats the averages. The point is that the precise psychological processes which make for success in all these fields are unknown and indeed unknowable in advance. The rules for developing a strategic vision of the company's future do not exist, any more than the rules for writing a symphony. The approach to setting objectives and performance standards, therefore, calls for considerable humility on the part of management, accepting that it is not a case of senior managers knowing best what to do.

Performance standards and objectives

It follows that the setting of performance standards, targets and objectives must, if it is to be at all useful as a process, be a joint activity, and that the objectives resulting from the process, while focusing primarily on the organisation's needs, should include an element which recognises the goals of the individual.

An excellent example of an approach which meets this criterion and which works well in practice is 3M's 15% rule. People engaged in development can devote 15% of their working time to pet projects of their own devising while focusing on company-sponsored official projects for the remaining 85%.

Appraisal, counselling, coaching, mentoring and giving feedback: the developmental approach to performance
The process of influencing the performance of highly talented people performing unprogrammable tasks is best described as developmental. It will involve a whole range of tools.

- **Appraisal.** By the individual of his or her own performance and by peers, as well as by others who have more experience or carry over-all responsibility for the individual's performance and development.
- **Coaching.** By the line manager or other appropriate persons.
- **Mentoring.** In the case of the really top talent, mentoring should involve the most senior line managers.
- **Providing feedback.** This can be done in a range of ways including subordinate and peer-group attitude surveys or ratings, psychometric test scores or opportunities to "calibrate" an individual's performance and achievements alongside people doing similar jobs in other organisations.

All these processes have in common the fact that they not only provide acceptable ways of appraising and influencing performance but are also means for developing the talent of the individual.

All the companies visited for the present study were operating some form of systematic performance appraisal, but in almost every case there were considerable reservations as to how effective it was in relation to the performance of the most talented people. In the words of one respondent: "I'd say if we'd really invented the performance appraisal then none of us should be working; we should be out there selling it." Another American human-resources vice-president's viewpoint was:

> "Personally, I'm not an advocate of the written performance appraisal. I believe that coaching on an ongoing basis has as much impact as waiting, once a year, to sit down and talk about everything. I would prefer to take an issue that has occurred and then sit down and talk to the individual about it at that point in time, about how we could have done it, maybe, differently."

Some companies were developing fresh or novel approaches. J.P. Morgan, for example, was in the process of introducing peer reviews. Merck has adapted its performance appraisal process to take account of differences in levels of performance by divisions of the organisation. As a general rule only 5% of staff can be rated at the highest assessed performance level. If the division as a whole has been rated exceptional, however, that division can include more than 5% of its people in the top-rated category. The idea is that if your division is on top you had some part in putting it there so you deserve a greater than average chance of getting a top-level performance rating.

Harnessing talent: the competency approach

In the late 1970s in the USA the American Management Association (AMA) instigated a study to answer the question: "What are the characteristics that distinguish superior performance by working managers?" The study was carried out by consultants McBer Associates and the findings, published in 1982 by Richard Boyatzis,[4] attracted international attention. In the UK they were taken up by the government's training agency which applied them to management development and led to the setting up of the so-called Management Charter Initiative (MCI). The AMA definition of competency relates closely to the issue of harnessing talent to activities leading to practical achievements; competence is seen as an underlying characteristic of a manager causally related to superior performance on the job. The MCI uses the term more broadly to refer to the ability to perform a job in all its aspects to certain defined standards (rather than to exceptional standards). The MCI approach also includes those aspects of personal qualities and effectiveness that are required in the workplace to deal with co-workers, managers and customers.

Several companies have used a competency-based approach both to identify and to develop superior performance. Mostly this has been done in respect of managerial jobs, although some companies include specialists. The three case studies which follow illustrate different competency-based systems.

CASE STUDIES

The Hewlett Packard system

Hewlett Packard has developed a competency-based approach over the past 3–4 years. This has involved identifying the high-performance differentiators for key jobs. Both high performers and average performers have been interviewed with the objective of identifying what the differentiators are. The focus has been on the behavioural differences, namely what people actually do differently in the job.

The HP approach, although highly analytical and elaborate, is specifically designed to avoid problems of rigidity often associated with a competencies approach. Instead of just saying a high performer does more coaching, for example, the specific behavioural characteristic is defined: a high performer doing more coaching organises regular meetings with his or her people weekly, as opposed to every six months. Each competency is backed up, in the database, by a specific description of that competency in action, in a number of different jobs. This enables managers to produce an unlimited number of uniquely different job descriptions.

> "So unlike the British Charter Initiative and other approaches, where you say these are the competencies associated with being a manager, what we say is 'What do you want to get done in a job?', and then these are the competencies that help you describe what the job is. And the priority of those competencies is going to vary manager by manager, situation by situation, country by country. That's why we went for a very flexible system that is driven by the user."

Hewlett Packard has recently developed a software tool which allows groups of managers to profile jobs and identify the key development needs associated with them. The objective over the next few years is to enable individual employees to access the system before they discuss career development and performance issues with their manager so that they can do some "What if?" scenarios. "What happens if I stay in my present job?" "What skills will I need to develop?" or "I've got these skills, what jobs could I do?"

Hewlett Packard has also developed a generic model for doing competency modelling. It has three options involving varying depths of analysis and related costs. The simplest approach involves using the model with a group of managers familiar with a particular job and working on it for perhaps three hours or so. The "power" version involves going out and interviewing people in depth, doing full "critical incident" interviewing, coding the transcripts, and so on. This is a process that can take 3–4 months, involving significant cost. It is reserved for the key positions. The middle course is to work with a selected number of high-performing people and in the course of a number of group meetings pull out much the same data but in less analytical detail. The results are then validated with a wider group of people and the whole project is completed within 3–6 weeks.

The British Airways system

BA has been a leading company in the UK in its use of the management competency approach, which it employs as the basis for assessment of potential, determination of training and development needs and the setting of standards. Its approach is based on the chief executive's view that "to achieve the competitive edge we must ensure that all our personal talents are utilised to their highest possible potential".

As well as position-specific competencies the company has developed broad corporate-wide competencies which define what is expected in the way of standards at various management levels.

The level of most relevance to the present study is the senior-management level, at which the most talented among the managerial population can be expected to arrive. BA recognises that the work and the skills of senior managers are very much more nebulous than those at other levels of management and are, therefore, much harder to define and identify. It took a group of 24 of the most senior and most successful managers and, using them as a model of good practice and desired performance characteristics, developed a set of competencies against which the performance of other actual and potential senior managers can be assessed.

The seven primary competencies of senior general managers in British Airways to emerge from this process were as follows.

- **Vision.** The ability to develop innovative, well-informed coherent and future-oriented scenarios.
- **Direction.** The ability to generate strategies, plans and tactics based on a good assessment of priorities, facts, risks and possibilities.
- **Business orientation.** A business attitude and business sense that permeates every decision and action.
- **Results orientation.** Driven to be in command, to have responsibility and achieve results, and to be champion to worthwhile causes.
- **Managing relations.** The personal qualities and interpersonal skills that promote open and constructive relations with superiors, subordinates, peers and people outside the department.
- **Resource management.** The ability and skill to determine needs and man-

age the acquisition and deployment of resources, both human and physical, in a business-like way.
- **Large organisation perspective.** An appreciation of and sensitivity to the complex interdependencies in a large international airline.

Each of these is further elaborated by descriptions of the appropriate behaviours, an essential additional step if the competency approach is to be effective as a tool for performance management. The "Direction" competency, for example, involves the following.

1 Setting strategy
- Investigates relevant background, gathers necessary information.
- In thinking takes into account corporate goals, visions, department mission.
- Considers the options and selects a sound approach.

2 Planning courses for action
- Identifies necessary actions, in sensible sequence, by whom, and with an appropriate sense of timescales.
- Identifies possible contingencies and makes allowances for these in planning and tactics.

3 Communication
- Communicates and wins support for strategy and plan with relevant stakeholders.
- Communicates the direction and takes steps to ensure understanding and support with own unit/department.

4 Managing the plan
- Builds in checkpoints, control mechanisms.
- Monitors progress against the plan, constantly readjusting it depending on circumstances.

Altogether the seven competencies embrace a total of 64 desired behaviours, which is an apt illustration of the complexity of the performance characteristics of high-level jobs. A similar approach, the Management Activities Profile, has been used by IBM for some years. Implemented globally and at all levels of management from first line to director, it lists 57 key management areas in ten broad groupings covering such subjects as communication, motivation and consideration, sub-divided into five "task" factors and five "people" factors. (This approach is different from almost all others, however, in the fact that the assessment is carried out by subordinates and is used only if the manager concerned agrees to its use.)

The United Technologies system

An example of a competency-based approach to "hybrids" as distinct from purely managerial work was provided by United Technologies. This has involved, in one division, a process known as "creating templates". The aim is to define the competencies required of engineering managers at various levels, including not only disciplines unique to engineering but also such aspects of the job as competence in the manufacturing area or in customer relations. These are assembled as "templates" and shared among the employees so that no one is left in doubt as to the standards of competency they will be required to meet. The templates cover some competencies which are deemed mandatory for a particular level along with others which are desirable.

The method used has been to look at profiles of successful, indeed "exceptional", performers and to compare them with those who have been less successful and to analyse the differences. In addition an attempt has been made to look to the future and identify future demands that changes in market conditions or other factors are likely to generate and to build these into the competencies, so that the danger of simply repeating in the future what proved successful in the past can, to a degree, be avoided.

For a high-technology company this approach is seen as very much a "soft science" but nevertheless as worth pursuing. The aim is to follow through and do the same with marketing jobs, purchasing jobs and others.

Nurturing talent: dealing with stress, crisis and burn-out

The achievements and levels of performance of highly talented people reflect a number of aspects of the whole person besides the possession of a particular set of abilities or aptitudes. These include self-confidence, emotional tone (optimism versus depression), tolerance of stress and physical and mental health. There is plenty of evidence from biographical studies to the effect that the working lives of talented people are rarely free from crises or setbacks arising from problems falling under one or other of these headings. When such situations arise they call for particularly sensitive handling and although it is a prime responsibility of line management to identify problems of this kind, the level of counselling skill required to resolve them is normally only found in those who have made it their professional field of work. For many US companies in particular the answer lies in adopting an Employee Assistance Programme, a personnel policy which enables employees, in confidence, to seek professional counselling and help when faced with some kind of crisis in their lives. Such programmes, when introduced, are used to an extent which surprises even those who perceived the need and advocated their introduction.

The most difficult case, however, is the individual who fails to seek help – whether from the EAP or the personnel department and/or the line manager – because of a denial of the problem, and in particular a refusal to face facts and accept that for whatever reason a significant deterioration in performance has occurred.

Companies differed both in the extent to which they recognised and faced up to issues of stress and "burn-out" in respect of their most talented people and also in the extent to which they had adopted appropriate strategies for dealing with it.

In one major UK financial services company the problem had been squarely faced and processes were in place to deal with it in co-operation with a counselling service known as Future Perfect. Career crisis problems were faced in such a way that the spouse of the individual concerned was involved at an early stage.

Stress in the financial services sector is probably most pronounced in the dealing activity, where a combination of relentless pressure to achieve, long working hours, substantial penalties for failure and work which is not in itself very intrinsically satisfying make for an overall work situation that few people can cope with indefinitely. In one such company the personnel function performed a therapeutic role to some extent, providing counselling. Nevertheless the personnel manager took the view that "burn-out" was unavoidable and would occur in most cases after 10–20 years in the job.

Another personnel director in a scientific environment expressed the view that the company was reluctant to face up to stress. "There are, literally, people going bonkers." This company had introduced an Employee Assistance Programme, the impact of which was described as "dramatic". The service had been used by 7% of employees within the first three months.

The chief executive of another UK financial services group expressed the view that there is a huge amount of waste of talent in UK industry due to problems of career crisis. His company's approach was to deal with such problems by counselling and providing support. He spent a substantial proportion of his own time in this way.

One US company endeavours to promote self-management and overall health. People are encouraged to take their full vacation entitlements. However:

> "The reality is that there are more encouragements within the system for the high potentials to stay driven, and that's how they continue to distinguish themselves. Many such people seem to adapt to it, that is until they retire and then die of a heart attack."

SUMMARY

The central problem in the field of performance management as it affects the most talented people in organisations is to reconcile commercial effectiveness with the flourishing of creative ability. Thus performance management is more to do with influence than direction.

Such an approach requires top management to abandon ideas about productivity of the kind pioneered by Frederick W. Taylor and to develop more subtle approaches based on a deep understanding of the factors which affect the performance of the most talented among their employees.

Such individuals bring a level of talent which exists as potential, together with a set of personal qualities and a pattern of needs or drives. They also contribute responsibility for their own self-development. The organisation's task is to create an overall framework within which talent can flourish. Given this, the next step is to identify talent wherever it exists. Performance standards or targets need to be set and a range of processes such as appraisal, counselling, coaching and mentoring put in place. Appropriate incentives, rewards and other motivational programmes must be developed. Finally, the organisation must invest in the continued development of talent.

Setting performance standards requires the reconciliation of the needs of the organisation for commercial success with the desired work and career objectives of talented persons. In addition the process must be based upon acceptance of the fact that most of the work they perform is unprogrammable and that in consequence it is not capable of being precisely specified either as to methods or outputs. Setting standards must, therefore, be a joint activity if it is to be effective.

Once standards have been agreed the monitoring of performance calls for a judicious blend of formal appraisal, counselling, coaching and the provision of feedback. These processes are undergoing active development and refinement among the companies taking part in this study. Few believe they have approached anything like perfection.

The approach which has gained in popularity during the late 1980s and early 1990s is the so-called "competencies" approach, pioneered by the American Management Association and based on the work of Boyatzis. The method has been used primarily in relation to managerial work rather than professional, scientific or technical tasks. It is based on the idea of trying to identify those behavioural characteristics which distinguish superior from average performance or the characteristic behaviours which will be required of effective senior executives as distinct from middle level or junior managers.

Companies are increasingly becoming sensitive to the impact of stress and pressure on the performance of talented people and are providing additional counselling services, mainly external to the company, to cope with "burn-out" and career crises.

References

1 Frederick W. Taylor, *Scientific Management*, New York, Harper and Row, 1947.

2 Peter Drucker, *Managing for the Future*, Oxford, Butterworth Heinemann, 1992.

3 Robert Levering, Milton Moskowitz and Michael Katz, *The 100 Best Companies to work for in America*, (Addison) Reading Mass., Addison Wesley Publishing Company, 1984.

4 R.E. Boyatzis, *The Competent Manager: A Model for Effective Performance*, New York, John Wiley, 1982.

7

HOW TALENTED PEOPLE ARE MOTIVATED

Psychologists distinguish between intrinsic and extrinsic motivation. The former refers to the drive to engage in a particular behaviour, while the latter refers to the motivating force of the consequences of engaging in the activity.

The importance of intrinsic motivation

Modern theories hold that intrinsic motivation is much the more powerful of the two, particularly in the case of highly talented and creative people, who will achieve most when motivated primarily by the interest and challenge of the work itself.

Research has shown that such people are more likely to be creative when there are no expectations of extrinsic rewards and that where expectations of such rewards are created they can exert a negative effect, as people try to gain them with as little effort as possible.[1] If a person who is intrinsically interested in a task is given substantial external rewards as well, his or her behaviour may begin to be controlled by the reward rather than the intrinsic interest.

Intrinsically motivated activity is activity which is an end in itself; extrinsically motivated behaviour is directed towards some external goal such as a financial reward. Intrinsic motivation is associated with goals that people set for themselves, and satisfies personal needs. The idea of doing something as an end in itself has been called functional autonomy by Allport,[2] who applied the concept to creative activity of the kind engaged in by research scientists. He believed, indeed, that it was not possible for creative activity to be extrinsically motivated.

For creative people goals may be self-generated (beating their past record), or reflect their underlying values (doing something which will benefit mankind), or arise from accepting and identifying with a group or organisation. In this sense talented people who are primarily motivated by the desire to do their best to assist their organisation to beat the competition may be said to be intrinsically motivated.

The value of moderate freedom

In order to improve the level of creative achievement, therefore, companies may need to be very cautious about concrete rewards. Glassman[3] argues that managers should "stop distracting R&D professionals with external motivators like salary raises, bonuses and promotion". He goes on to emphasise that salary raises, bonuses and promotion cannot, of course, be dispensed with – it is a matter of emphasis – but should be treated as reinforcing agents rather than as the foundations of motivation. He asked 200 R&D people in five *Fortune 500* corporations what were the biggest obstacles to creativity in their job environment and what they needed to be more creative. The most important factor to emerge from the study was the need for more time and more freedom. Research evidence from a number of studies, however, shows that R&D scientists in industry who were most effective in terms of both contributions to scientific knowledge and usefulness to the organisation were neither tightly nor loosely but moderately controlled. In other words, complete freedom of choice as to how to allocate their time or what to focus on is not as conducive to creative output as moderate freedom involving consultation and joint decision-making with managers.

It is clear that some talent-intensive organisations have successfully learned how to motivate talented people and have improved their competitive position accordingly. There are some excellent examples among the companies taking part in the present research. It is equally clear, however, that other companies still operate with an outmoded approach.

The common corporate error

In such organisations people of exceptional talent, on whose salaries and benefits business is expending huge sums, are considered to be sufficiently motivated to achieve and to work in the company's interests under conditions which reflect traditional custom and practice in the more labour-intensive firms of the past.

There is, in such cases, a failure to face up to the problem of how to motivate the professional so as to obtain his or her maximum commitment and output. A key part of the problem is to do with the ethos of professionalism, involving the integrity of professional values and conduct, and the need to test and to renew professional knowledge. Professionals live in two worlds: the internal world of the enterprise in which they find themselves treated as a resource; and the external world of professional associations, allegiances and networks in which they are often judged on quite different criteria.

In Drucker's view the traditional motivators – extrinsic rewards such as pay, pensions and related benefits, stock options, bonuses, and so on – do not work with highly talented personnel. Dissatisfaction with such matters may destroy motivation, but satisfaction with them very quickly becomes taken for granted and ceases to have a positive impact on motivation. Such people need a sense of achievement, a challenge, to know what their contribution is. They are not looking for the traditional fair day's pay for a fair day's work but, given the right conditions, they are looking for opportunities to do an exceptional day's work. They expect that the demands placed upon them will be ones which arise from the task or from the disciplines of professionalism rather than the demands of the boss.[4]

Knowledge does not acknowledge the existence of any authority other than that residing within the body of knowledge itself. In the values system of the professional, superficial knowledge bows to in-depth knowledge, and obsolescent knowledge bows to up-to-date knowledge; knowledge per se does not bow to organisational authority. Similarly, skill accepts the authority which derives from superior skill but not that which is based on superior rank or status.

The outcome of motivation

It is useful to distinguish between two possible outcomes of a high level of motivation. One is strong identification with, and positive commitment to, a particular organisation. The stronger this is, the higher the retention rate of highly talented personnel. The second is outstanding performance. Although many of the same factors will influence both outcomes, there are some important differences. It is consequently important for organisations to think through distinct strategies for retention and for motivation in respect of job performance. Indeed, in diagnosing motivational problems the simple matrix in Figure 2 may be a useful analytical tool.

Retention of talented personnel

It is easier to solve the problem of retention than it is to solve the more complex problems surrounding performance motivation. Retention issues tend to peak at two stages. The first is following induction, early training and one or two job assignments. At this stage the individual has acquired greater value in the open market and will be looking to exploit this. At the same time he or she will be looking for opportunities

Figure 2 **The motivational matrix**

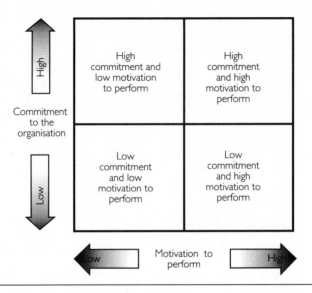

to apply the knowledge and experience that has been acquired and to be given responsibility and challenge. A third factor will be the extent to which experience to date with this first employer has or has not met the expectations created on entry and the aspirations of the individual.

A UK study[5] of the early work experience of graduates highlighted a number of problems.

- Failure to set clear objectives for graduate recruitment in the first place. (Now we have got them, what are we going to do with them?)
- Where selection is based on the objective of identifying long-term potential, a lack of clarity about the nature and purpose of assignments in the early years. These were described by one personnel manager as "ways of filling in the time until they become mature enough to be given real responsibility".
- Difficulties to do with the transition from education to work; the process of change and maturation on the part of individuals resulting in changing aspirations and priorities, both for their careers and for their lives generally.
- Frequency of moves in the first few years.

A US study[6] illustrated how attitudes can change in the first few years of employment. After working for 1–5 years graduates placed much more emphasis on "quality of life" needs, such as time for reflection, flexible working hours and the opportunity to attend conferences and courses, than they had on entry, at which point factors such as salary, company location and career prospects were more important.

When questioned about retention policies in relation to young entrants companies responded in a variety of ways. One type of response was to indicate that retention was not a problem and to explain why. The explanation rarely included being the company in the industry offering the highest salary and related benefits, although above average material rewards featured as an important factor in most cases. J.P. Morgan was one such company.

CASE STUDIES

J.P. Morgan

J.P. Morgan reported an attrition rate at around 10% per annum, low relative to its competitors. The success of the organisation and the challenging nature of the jobs were believed to contribute to this. Also:

> "People genuinely like the people they are working with. This is not a 'sharp elbow' organisation; you're not expected to crawl over other people to get to the top. . . . Another factor is the organisation structure; we have deliberately kept it flat. . . . This means two things, people get real decision-making responsibility at a very early age . . . and secondly it de-emphasises the hierarchical aspects of the organisation and people therefore concentrate much more on the professional satisfaction they are getting from their activities. I would say that the main thing that continues to drive them now is the changing nature of the organisation: the changing products, the evolutionary nature of our business, the new opportunities that we can provide them with through the growth of our business."

It was suggested that in many other firms the talented person would have to move outside to do something different. In J.P. Morgan they would probably be asked to do it anyway, with changes on offer both by job and by national location.

SAS Institute

In the US software house SAS Institute, the retention policy, which was proving eminently successful, is based on seven key points.

- Everyone is treated as special; we try to satisfy their individual desires and needs as far as possible without creating chaos within the organisation.
- All staff, from facilities and maintenance people up to the company president, enjoy the same benefits plan. There is no differentiation when it comes to the profit-sharing plan, for example; every full-time employee is eligible for an annual bonus, calculated on the earned income of the individual for the previous year.
- An open job-posting system. Approved and legitimate positions within the company are posted for all employees to see and apply for if they wish. Clearly, applicants would have to be suitably qualified and go through an interview process, but the system is open.
- Very good health and fitness facilities are available.
- The number of rules and constraints are kept to an absolute minimum. The personnel function prides itself on keeping the company policies and procedures down to one modest ringbinder file.
- There is not the usual tension between "management" and "staff" and the personnel function maintains an open-door policy. Employee input is very important and is taken seriously; many changes in personnel policies over the years have been initiated by employee suggestions. "We try to do things that are common sense."
- The organisation is not status conscious; for example, there are no reserved parking places for anyone (except for service vehicles), no executive washrooms or special dining rooms, and so on. Hence staff get to see the very senior people on a regular basis. Much business is done at lunch or at the recreation and fitness centre as a result.

This is a clear example of an organisation with an approach to retention based on largely non-material rewards and tailored to the perceived values systems of the professional staff in question.

Colgate Palmolive

In Colgate Palmolive retention policy is based on three supporting planks: career development, compensation plans and job factors.

"Probably the most important factor in retention is the ability to deliver on their own career aspirations (assuming that those aspirations are realistic). We try to ensure that someone in addition to their own boss is having discussions with them about career goals, and that they are the individuals who are being given career opportunities within the company."

The company is conscious of the importance of money, however. The "very highest potential people" are said to get very careful reviews of their compensation. With a modest average annual salary increase at present, emphasis is placed on bonuses. High potentials are usually achieving well or overachieving against their targets for bonus payments, and may get stock awards even before having reached the official level.

"But probably the most powerful dynamic is what people get to do on a job, and the kind of attention they get from senior management."

The company's strong internal culture was also instanced as a reason for its very low staff turnover in general and of high potential people in particular.

Solvay

In the international chemical company Solvay, with its head-office base in Belgium, a high retention rate is attributed to a number of factors, including the name of the company and the implied security and stability going along with that; good salaries and benefits (not the best in the industry but in the top quartile); and career prospects (considered to be perhaps the most important factor). The policy is to give graduate entrants challenging tasks immediately on joining, and to test and develop them. If the response is good they are then sent outside Belgium as soon as possible, or at least moved to a new position within the country; mobility is more or less mandatory.

Thomson

In the French company Thomson the question of retention is approached in a systematic way at the end of an individual's first three years in the company. At this point each person is interviewed with the purpose of discovering whether they wish to stay with the company and make a career. The manager will also have a view on the potential of the individual to develop and make a contribution. If agreement is reached on both sides that he or she should stay for a career then steps are taken to provide more information about the company and to integrate the individual more fully within it.

The main method for achieving this is the Three Year Convention. This is a week-long gathering of young people from all parts of the business and from all over the world. About 150 people attend. They meet the top managers of the company and the chairman and chief executive officer explain the strategy and answer questions. There are opportunities for the young people to present their activities to their colleagues. They also visit plants, engage in small group activities and in social occasions. These conventions started three years before the present research and four are held every year. After the experience people understand more and feel that they belong.

Steps which improve retention of graduates

The UK study referred to above by the Institute of Manpower Studies[7] resulted in a number of recommended steps likely to improve a company's ability to choose graduates successfully and retain those it wished to. The main recommendations were as follows.

- Establish a corporate policy for graduate recruitment based on a realistic assessment of the numbers needed, with a clear allocation of the roles to be played by line management at corporate and at local level in the operation of the policy. The policy should be clearly communicated to the recruits.
- Avoid creating inflated expectations about jobs and career opportunities.
- First jobs should be interesting, involve real work, some chance to use initiative and carry responsibility. The new entrant should be the responsibility of a supportive line manager and not imposed on a reluctant sponsor.

- The rationale for selecting the early sequence of jobs or placements should reflect a planned experience which will meet the needs of the business on the one hand while leaving some room for flexibility and the exercise of choice on the part of the individual on the other.
- Ensure that there is full communication of career options and opportunities and regular, frequent feedback about process, performance and potential.
- Provide relevant training and real support for those undergoing further study for professional qualifications or advanced qualifications of various kinds.
- Provide "third party" support and guidance. Ideally senior line managers should be given training and be willing to serve as mentors for young beginners.
- Effect a smooth transition between the end of the first period of training mixed with planned experience and the first "real" job. This should involve consideration of the individual's preferences.
- Monitor the success (including the retention rate) of the graduate entry process. Investigate the reasons for attrition systematically.
- Be flexible. As needs and priorities change in the business and as the individuals themselves develop and change attitudes or preferences it is important to be prepared to adjust plans accordingly.

Retention of key, experienced personnel

The problems of retention of top level personnel in key positions are somewhat different from those involved in the case of young entrants. In most cases the individuals whose knowledge, skill or competence are critical for the success of an organisation will be targeted by competitors, either directly or through executive search consultants. In many instances they will be called weekly or even more frequently. They will be offered attractive packages to entice them to leave for fresh pastures. All the firms involved in the present study were, of course, alert to the problem and a range of strategies was in use to deal with it.

A prominent factor of such strategies is to provide what are often described as "golden handcuffs": a package of rewards including high basic salary, bonuses, "top hat" pension and other benefits, and (above all) attractive stock options. Firms cannot afford to neglect paying attention to the competitive quality of their compensation packages but it is also widely perceived that a strategy based on material benefits alone is unlikely to prove effective. No matter how good the package a determined competitor can always beat it. It is also the case that there is now a global market for top talent, with the consequence that what are perceived as golden handcuffs in one country (for example, the UK where top people's pay is fiercely scrutinised and subject to hostile press comment) would be seen as tin handcuffs elsewhere.

A second strategy is to attempt to restrict mobility of key personnel by means of service contracts which contain clauses preventing employees from working for directly competing organisations within a specified period of time following their leaving their existing employer. Such contracts are notoriously difficult to enforce.

The third approach is to "grab them by their hearts as well as by the wallet"; that is, to build loyalty, cohesion and identification with the organisation. This third approach is seen as the most effective by most of the organisations in the present research. It is clearly exemplified by the case of IBM's Don Estridge, described by Frank Rose in *West of Eden*.[8]

When IBM decided to go for the PC, Don Estridge, as a bright young software manager, was picked to head the project. Between 1980 and 1983 his unit grew from a 12-person task force to a fully fledged division of IBM. Estridge followed Apple's example with a highly entrepreneurial approach, breaking IBM rules, creating an atmosphere of excitement and challenge. Like Steve Jobs at Apple he was full of energy, charismatic, brilliant; he also had a very trusting and generous nature.

By the autumn of 1982 headhunters were very active. Estridge was invited to California, where he spent a full day in meetings with the president of Apple. Later he and his wife met Steve Jobs back in Florida. Apple was offering a package worth several million dollars, more than he or anyone else could hope to make in IBM. Yet, after long talks with IBM head office at Armonk, he decided to stay.

Why? He and his team had set out to build a machine to beat Apple; he did not like the idea of, in effect, deserting to the opposition. More important, however, was the thought that when people asked him where he worked he enjoyed saying "IBM".

Motivation and performance

In the quest for a deeper understanding of the values and motivation of its own key personnel, one major UK knowledge-intensive enterprise sponsored a research project. At the time the company was reviewing the compensation package for the top 2,500 people and enlisted the assistance of a research team drawn jointly from the UK business school, Ashridge, and the Centre for the Utilisation of the Social

Sciences, Loughborough University.

The team carried out by interview and questionnaire a wide-ranging study which included obtaining attitudes and opinions on current personnel policies and methods of remuneration. Nevertheless the study of motivation was seen as the central plank of the project, recognising that a system of rewards which fails to take account of individual differences in motivation cannot be wholly effective.

The study covered all staff at middle and senior levels in the UK with the sole exception of main board directors; directors of subsidiaries and divisions were included. The people were drawn from 11 different organisational units (subsidiary companies or product divisions) in 110 locations. They were in a range of jobs including general management, functional management and such specialised fields as licensing, research, insurance and public affairs.

At the time of the study the existing system of rewards was showing signs of strain. Although a number of ad hoc modifications had been made over the years this patching up process had made the system increasingly complex and difficult to administer. At the same time preliminary soundings of opinion had already indicated that there was no consensus as to what changes to the system were desirable. On the contrary, there was a wide range of different ideas and suggestions, reflecting the very great range of needs which individuals were seeking to satisfy at work.

Following a set of pilot interviews with various groups of staff in different locations a carefully designed questionnaire was sent to all 2,500 staff in the appropriate job grades. No fewer than 2,246 or 90% were returned for analysis.

In general terms the survey results showed that although the great majority of respondents were reasonably well satisfied with the company as an employer, there were significant problems. A commonly expressed need was for a closer link between remuneration and individual performance and a concern that there were only marginal differences in remuneration between outstanding and below-average performers, despite the fact that the compensation system included an elaborate mechanism designed to correct this. The complexity of the scheme, coupled with failings of communication, had in fact resulted in its being incompletely understood. The performance appraisal system was seen as uneven in both quality and the extent of its application from one part of the company to another. There was a frequently expressed desire for much greater flexibility and recognition of the differing needs and circumstances of individuals instead of the uniform company-wide approach imposed from the centre.

Asked to indicate the desirable characteristics of an effective compensation package, strongest support was given to the need to recognise individual differences – in performance as well as need and circumstances – to openness and to flexibility, both of operation and in respect of the form in which individuals could receive their benefits. On other issues, however, opinions were often sharply divided; for example, on the question of whether or not the company should seek to maintain the existing differentials between the various grades of employee. There was, in sum, no simple consensus.

During the interview stage it soon became evident that there was a wide range of needs which individuals were seeking to satisfy through their work. Some spoke of working primarily for a level of material reward sufficient to support a particular lifestyle they wished to attain or maintain for themselves and their families. Others put more emphasis on other factors such as wanting to feel they were making a worthwhile contribution to the company or that they were being stretched or challenged in their work or were getting the opportunity and facilities to work in their own chosen specialist field. Most respondents mentioned several things that were important to them rather than just one and it was interesting to note that many also added, unbidden, that they had little or no interest in certain rewards which they perceived their colleagues as valuing highly.

This rich interview material pointed to the fact that there is considerably more variation in motivation between individuals than is allowed for in most of the well-known theories of motivation. Certainly the evidence emphasised that there is no one motivational blueprint for all people, not even for all managers. On the other hand some people clearly have a lot in common with some others and it was decided to attempt to identify groups or clusters of people whose motivational patterns, if not identical, were clearly similar. With this aim in mind, the crucial part of the questionnaire was designed. In this, respondents were asked to rate, on a seven-point scale, the importance they placed on each of 31 satisfactions or rewards, some tangible and some intangible.

Some of the satisfactions were scored highly by many or most of the respondents, particularly those like autonomy, self-fulfilment and achievement. Other satisfactions which tended to attract high scores generally were "the feeling of making a worthwhile contribution to the division or company", "recognition for hard work and good performance" and "the amount of money you are paid in terms of the spending power it gives you".

Other satisfactions, however, showed marked differences in scoring; examples included "your reputation in your profession or career field", status and prestige, and the amount of free time.

The relative importance attached to the rewards by each respondent was then subjected to statistical processing using a form of cluster analysis to see if there were, indeed, identifiable groups or clusters of executives the members of which shared closely similar patterns of need.

The analysis in fact threw up six clear-cut groups. Each group had a marked tendency to share common views both about the rewards they regarded as of prime importance and those they regarded as of little importance, relative to their colleagues in other groups.

The six groups are shown in Figure 3. In this diagram, based on a computer plot of clusters of data, the members of any one group had most in common with each other, then some common ground with the groups adjacent to them, but least in common with the group opposite. The six groups were found to be significantly different from each other, not only in terms of their motivational pattern, but also in relation to a whole range of other characteristics such as age, length of service, function or section of the company. Again, those in adjacent groups were found to have more in common than those on opposite sides of the diagram. The statistical analysis showed that 92% of those who completed the questionnaire shared one of the six motivational patterns. (The remainder appeared either undecided or may have answered the questionnaire more or less randomly.)

Group 1 The drive for material reward. This was the largest of the groups, accounting for about 25% of the sample population. They rated highly such rewards as spending power, fringe benefits affording tax advantages, opportunities to accumulate capital and continuing opportunities for promotion and advancement.

Relatively unimportant were opportunities for free time, having congenial colleagues or a job with a high degree of intellectual or vocational interest.

This group was somewhat younger on average and more inclined to be mobile in search of career opportunities. The production management and finance functions were strongly represented in this group while very few research scientists had much in common with them.

Figure 3 **Six Motivational Groups**

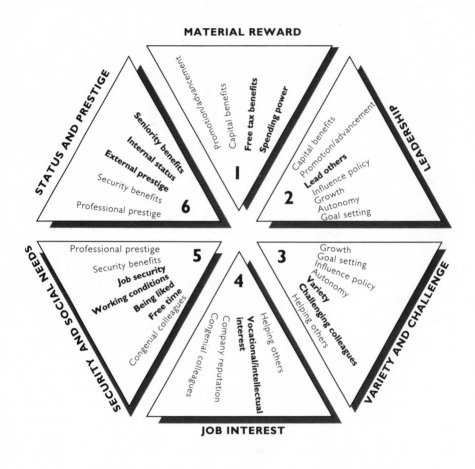

MATERIAL REWARD

STATUS AND PRESTIGE

LEADERSHIP

SECURITY AND SOCIAL NEEDS

VARIETY AND CHALLENGE

JOB INTEREST

Promotion/advancement
Capital benefits
Free tax benefits
Spending power

1

Seniority benefits
Internal status
External prestige
Security benefits
Professional prestige

6

Capital benefits
Promotion/advancement
Lead others
Influence policy
Growth
Autonomy
Goal setting

2

Professional prestige
Security benefits
Job security
Working conditions
Being liked
Free time
Congenial colleagues

5

Growth
Goal setting
Influence policy
Autonomy
Variety
Challenging colleagues
Helping others

3

4

Helping others
Vocational/intellectual interest
Company reputation
Congenial colleagues

Group 2 The drive for leadership and power. This smaller group (6% of the total) was made up of those with a particularly strong need to be in charge, to lead others and, related to this, to have continuing opportunities for promotion, personal growth, autonomy, a feeling of being at the centre of things and able to influence policy. They showed little interest in being popular with colleagues or having pleasant working conditions. They were, on average, the youngest group, were more likely than other groups to be in production or marketing management jobs and were the most potentially mobile.

Group 3 The drive for variety, achievement and challenge. This group, 10% of the sample population as a whole, were distinguishable from their colleagues by the strong emphasis they placed on such factors as variety of tasks, and having challenging colleagues of high calibre, combined with a virtually complete lack of concern with status.

As in the case of Group 1 they were younger than average although not as young as Group 2. They were well represented in production management and personnel jobs.

Group 4 The drive for job or vocational interest. This group included 15% of the sample population. They attached particularly high importance to having a job the content of which met their personal vocational or intellectual interests. They rated monetary rewards as relatively unimportant and they were less ambitious than those in Groups 1–3. People with this outlook were likely to be found working in research and development, information technology or personnel.

Group 5 The drive for security and comfort. 18% of the staff gave high ratings to such satisfactions as those associated with job security, good working conditions and congenial colleagues. This was by far the oldest and most long-serving group.

Group 6 The drive for status. For 19% the status associated with their position in the company, together with the benefits and "perks" that went with status, were of major importance. (This, perhaps, is a particularly British source of motivation.) Strongly represented in this group were people in the professional specialisations concerned with legal matters, licensing, insurance, planning and public affairs.

Respondents were also asked to what extent the various types of satisfaction were to be found in their present jobs. Only two groups – those seeking job interest and security – were pretty well satisfied. Those in Groups 1 and 2 were particularly likely to be dissatisfied.

The attitudes of the six groups to different approaches to compensation also varied. Groups 1 and 2 (material reward and leadership) gave above average support to rewarding performance (of teams as well as individuals), to openness about the basis for remuneration, flexibility to allow for special cases, scope for individual choice and the use of fringe benefits. Group 3 (variety and challenge) looked for clarity and openness and preferred a basis in job evaluation.

Group 4 (job interest) looked for remuneration to reflect the profitability of the organisation as a whole rather than individual or sectional performance, and preferred material rewards exclusively in money rather than a mix of cash and fringe benefits. Group 5 (security and comfort) supported ease of administration, annual increments to reflect length of service, money rather than fringe benefits and the maintenance of existing differentials.

Group 6 (status) favoured a simple, easily understood system, annual service increments, fringe benefits and the maintenance of differentials.

These patterns will, of course, reflect both the UK culture and the particular corporate culture of the company at the time the research was carried out. Nevertheless, the implications for the present study are clear. Different types of qualified and talented personnel do have different needs and values and, therefore, are motivated in different ways. The biggest issue is clearly that creative people function in different ways and they have different priorities. "Not to make money. What they want most is creative perfection. This leads to tension; we need to find the right balance. We get on much better these days. I've learned to see their side a bit more." Managers, in particular, are motivated in quite different ways from research scientists and (equally important in its implications) are likely to have difficulty in understanding how research scientists feel.

One chief executive interviewed was quite convinced he knew what motivated the computer software experts in his organisation: "Salary comes first, culture second, and you like the people you work with, third." There was unfortunately no opportunity to test his opinions by asking the people themselves.

Three of the companies interviewed offered particularly interesting insights into motivation.

CASE STUDIES

Merck

Merck is one company which has given much thought to motivating professional staff. A reward limited to very substantial accomplishments, the Directors' Scientific Award, is regarded as a very high honour. It involves a monetary gift, substantial public recognition and the opportunity to designate a school or institution to which the company makes a sizeable contribution on the recipient's behalf.

There is also a programme which rewards substantial innovation by stock options which are "event driven" rather than "time driven". For example, an innovation in basic research may attract a grant of a stock option which can only be exercised as the innovation moves through the pipeline into manufacturing. The process is phased, with a percentage of the grant being able to be exercised at various stages of product development and testing, with 100% being contingent upon a new product moving into the market.

United Technologies

United Technologies is another company which clearly recognises the need to get better at managing what they call the "high pros" or the top professionals.

> "You rely on them and you make significant investments in those people in the way of training and development, but our systems have tended to be focused toward the management side in terms of compensation, recognition and visibility".

A hypothetical example was quoted of a person who might be a world-class expert in high-temperature alloys, working alone or in a small group, perhaps on blade technology. That individual might never manage the blade programme and will never manage engine development; it is not what interests them, not what they have been trained to do. "But our hierarchy tends to pay for upward mobility instead of competency in a real technical sense. I think it's time we really adapted our compensation schemes to people like that."

The point was made that to do so will require even more careful management of people to achieve truly improved technical contributions, not just the status quo.

Rockwell

In Rockwell as well recognition is emphasised. The company operates several recognition programmes including the "Engineer of the Year" award which involves selecting engineers throughout the world who have made significant contributions and flying each one, together with spouse, to a three-day event, during which they are presented with their awards by the chairman of the board. The programme provides a lot of highly visible recognition; the winners' pictures and names are published in the major US engineering publications.

Specific motivators for highly talented personnel

In the course of the interviews for this project the issue of motivation was frequently raised. A wide range of specific motivators was mentioned as being of particular relevance in the case of highly talented, highly educated, professional personnel. A list of these motivators is given below.

- A strong sense of mission, of the worth of the company's goals.
- The integrity or high ethical standards of the organisation.
- Challenging assignments.
- Attractive career opportunities.
- Being a stockholder, owning shares in the business.
- An egalitarian, single status culture.
- A flat organisation structure with little hierarchy, little bureaucracy.
- An aesthetically pleasant, campus-like work environment.
- A sense of family within the business.
- Special awards and recognition programmes for technical achievement.
- Opportunity and encouragement to publish and to present papers at conferences and to take office in professional or scientific associations.
- Being an equal-opportunity employer.
- Providing a high level of autonomy and freedom.
- Respect for individuals.
- Cohesive work teams.
- Being associated with a business with a first class reputation in its field.
- Support for education programmes.

- Participative approach to decision-making.
- Programmes to alleviate stress and to provide counselling when needed.
- Leadership and example from top management.
- Being trusted.
- Fun occasions like "beer busts", spontaneous parties, and so on.
- No compulsory lay-offs.
- Flexible working hours.
- Openness in communications.
- "Cafeteria"-type compensation systems.

SUMMARY

Psychologists distinguish between intrinsic motivation, derived from the work itself, and associated satisfactions such as seeing work applied in a worthwhile cause, and extrinsic motivation which derives from external rewards such as pay, prizes, status, and so on. Modern theory holds that intrinsic motivation is much the more powerful, particularly so in the case of highly gifted people. It is widely accepted that the traditional motivators do not work at all well with the most highly talented personnel.

Motivation has two possible outcomes: the desire to remain with a particular organisation; and the desire to do a good job. Different processes are involved in these two areas.

Retention issues peak at two stages. The first is in the early years, following induction and the first one or two job assignments. Poor retention rates at this stage reflect a number of common problems, including the following.

- Failure to set clear objectives for graduate recruitment.
- Lack of a well thought-out policy for dealing with those of particularly high potential.
- The ways in which the individuals themselves change their priorities and aspirations during these early years when they are still maturing.
- The frequency of moves during this period.

Companies in the present study which were particularly successful in retaining their best people attributed the reasons to a number of factors. The reputation of the organisation, the challenge of assignments and career opportunities led the list. In retaining key senior personnel, loyalty to the organisation matters as much or more than compensation.

Studies of patterns of motivation have identified several distinct groups, with managers differing sharply from professional and scientific staff in their requirements.

References

1 Teresa M. Amabile and Stanley S. Gryskiewicz, *Creativity in the Research Laboratory*, Greensboro N.C., Center for Creative Leadership, 1987.
2 G.W. Allport, *Pattern and Growth in Personality*, New York, Hoch, Rinehorst and Winston, 1961.
3 E. Glassman, "Managing for Creativity: Back to Basics in R&D", *R&D Management*, 16, 2, 1986.
4 Peter Drucker, *The Age of Discontinuity*, London, Heinemann, 1969.
5 Helen Connor *et al.*, *You and Your Graduates: the First Few Years*, Brighton, Institute of Manpower Studies, 1990.
6 Ronald L. Cotterman, "How Recent Graduates View Their Jobs", *Research and Technology Management*, vol. 34, no. 3, May–June 1991.
7 Helen Connor, *op. cit.*
8 Frank Rose, *West of Eden*, London, Arrow Books, 1989.

8

THE ORGANISATIONAL FRAMEWORK FOR NURTURING TALENT

This chapter attempts to identify the characteristics of social institutions which are not only successful in attracting, retaining, nurturing and motivating highly talented people, but also outstandingly successful in the business sense.

Organisational design

The object of organisational design is the efficient utilisation of resources. Human resources are no exception. There are five main targets for designers to bear in mind under the human-resource heading.

1 Achieving an appropriate level of control over the activities of the organisation's members. The emphasis here is on the word appropriate.

Generally speaking, the more highly talented the workforce the more appropriate it is to use minimum controls. It is also generally the case that highly talented people resist and resent controls and do their best to subvert them.

2 Achieving an adequate degree of co-ordination and integration of people's activities in relation to the organisation's overall task. The work of talented elites has to be integrated with that of supporting personnel, and co-operation and mutual understanding has to be achieved between managers and specialists or between specialists in different disciplines.

3 Providing necessary and effective interfaces with key aspects of the organisation's environment: markets served, key customers within them and suppliers, including suppliers of capital. In the present context key issues include relationships with the scientific and technological community at large and with the universities and colleges as suppliers of talent.

4 Influencing levels of motivation and commitment, which involves creating the kind of organisational setting which channels intrinsic motivation in the direction of corporate goals.

5 Creating a climate within which innovation and creativity can flourish.

Structures, systems and cultures

In designing organisations there are three sets of tools to work with.

- **Structural tools.** These include job descriptions, different ways of grouping people in teams or divisions, spans of control, centralisation or decentralisation of functions, decisions about unit size, and so on.

- **Tools in the form of systems and procedures.** These are analogous to the physiology of organisms; they provide the flows of information which form the basis of decisions and action. There are systems and procedures for financial and cost control, systems for quality control, procedures for recruiting and selecting personnel and for performance appraisal, procedures for progressing jobs through from order to completion, procedures for launching new products, and so on.

- **Tools which fall under the general heading of corporate culture.** These correspond to the psychology of the organism. Under this heading fall such characteristics of organisations as sense of mission, shared values, characteristic management style and accepted ways of doing things.

In practice these three aspects are difficult to disentangle. They are, of course, closely interrelated; the kind of organisation described as "bureaucratic" will tend to have a hierarchical structure with centralised decision-making, elaborate formal systems and procedures covering virtually every aspect of organisational life and a set of values favouring order, efficiency, impersonality, integrity and conformity.

Table 1 shows how decisions about structure, choices of systems and procedures and the influences of corporate culture relate to the achievement of organisational objectives. This matrix can be used as a template for organisation design.[1]

Table I **A template for organisation design**

	Structure	Systems	Culture
Control	Hierarchy and span of control	Production control Stock control	Bureaucratic
Co-ordination and integration	Product divisionalisation Matrix structures	Integrated manu- facturing systems	Teamworking
Interface with environment	Market or geographical divisions Boundary roles	Environmental scanning Systematic consumer research	Outward-looking Market-oriented
Motivation	Autonomous work groups Job enrichment	Incentive schemes Employee share ownership schemes	Putting people first
Flexibility/ Innovation	Flat structures Interdisciplinary project teams	Special awards for innovation	Entrepreneurial Risk-taking

Structures and systems

Organisation as "social architecture"

Designing and building an enduring organisation involves creating a social institution to which people feel they belong and within which they are banded together by a sense of common purpose and shared values. It is no coincidence that so many of the world's great business corporations have given exceptional emphasis to this. For companies such as IBM, Hewlett Packard, Merck and L'Oréal the creation of a human organisation aspiring to certain ideals has been a key objective.

When the companies interviewed for this book were asked what characteristics an organisation required to attract and keep highly talented people, their replies almost always made more frequent reference to aspects of corporate culture than to the structural or systems characteristics of their organisations. When structure was referred to, the usual response was that talented people worked best in "flat" organisations.

> "Whenever creativity and innovation are involved, you cannot force people. . . . That is what is so interesting about businesses like this, because the power does not just belong with the top management, the power is everywhere in the company . . . that is what is exciting about companies like Thomson. . . . There used to be lots of layers, especially in that part of the company which deals with defence, too,

so they had a military view of organisation. But this is changing very fast . . . it's a very competitive business so you need to give more autonomy to people. That led us to organise on a more flexible basis, because a military-type organisation is particularly inadequate to face the competition."

Several organisations reported similar trends towards flat, less hierarchical structures. There was awareness that such structures offered less scope for career advancement of the traditional kind than hierarchical ones and that policies were needed to deal with this issue.

In the opinion of the vice-president of human resources of the Xerox Corporate Research Centre the answer lies in increasing the "value" of each employee. They should feel that they have market value to other companies as well as their own; "that they keep growing professionally". Coupled with that, there is a need for much more flexible compensation systems, so that people who cannot be promoted feel adequately rewarded.

A second structural feature mentioned was the motivating influence of cohesive, largely autonomous project groups or work teams, often in the context of matrix organisation structures which linked functional specialisations to market-driven projects. In GE-CGR the role of such teams was strongly emphasised.

"We need people able to work in teams, willing to work in a flexible organisation where you don't have a framework but you can adapt and change .... We are a matrix organisation so we want people who can work at the "crossroads" of different lines. . . . We may create a team for a specific project and there may be no one single leader with authority over every other member, so you have to help the team to learn how to design that, how to elect its own leader, its own 'scribe', its facilitator for the day, and so on."

Structure and innovation

Tom Peters and Nancy Austin[2] argue that we must learn to design organisations that take into account the "irreducible sloppiness" of the innovation process. They point out that most innovation occurs in unplanned, unpredictable ways, often in industries quite unrelated to the nature of the innovation. They quote the well-known study by John Jewkes who analysed 58 major inventions ranging from ballpoint pens to penicillin. At least 46 of these occurred in "the wrong place"; that is, in very small firms, by individuals, by people in "out-groups" in large firms or by people in large firms in the wrong industries. Examples include Kodachrome, invented by two musicians; continuous casting of steel discovered by a watchmaker experimenting with brass casting; synthetic detergents developed by dye-stuff chemists.

There is overwhelming evidence that much, if not most, new product innovation in big firms is the result of work by small groups of 6–24 people supported by a product champion but working in secret or in defiance of company policy or at least without official backing. Examples of such "skunkworks" are the development of the Axe digital switching system in Ericsson, AT&T's Unix operating system, the first locomotive built by GE and the development of the basic oxygen furnace by Nippon Kokan.

Decentralisation and delegation clearly foster innovation. Johnson and Johnson's phrase is "Growing big by staying small"; Hewlett Packard, 3M and Citicorp have similar approaches. For them, according to Peters, the structure is the strategy.

Another common structural feature of highly innovative firms is the close interaction between research, production and marketing people. Hewlett Packard has adopted the principle of the "triad" development team: design engineers, marketing and manufacturing people being full-time partners in product development from a very early stage.

Corporate culture

The report of the London Human Resource Group[3] drew attention to the key part played by corporate culture in high-talent organisations. It argued that significant cultural changes are needed in many institutions to lead to greater motivation of staff, and to pull the human-resource function towards meeting an identified business need. What is corporate culture and does it matter?

All organisations have a culture in the sense of a shared set of beliefs about how people should behave at work ("the way things are done around here") and a set of values concerned with defining the tasks and goals that really matter; for example, IBM's strong emphasis on respect for the individual. Values are often expressed in short, pithy phrases, such as the following.

- Universal service (AT&T).
- Putting people first (British Airways).
- Productivity through people (Dana Corporation).

In some cases, however, such slogans are mere advertising messages and do not accurately reflect the underlying culture of the firm. It is also the case that many companies with a strong, distinctive culture do not attempt to compress their values and beliefs into slogans.

Does culture make a difference in terms of the attitudes and motivation of employees and long-term competitiveness? That it does has always been an article of faith in IBM. Thomas Watson, its founder, held that "the basic philosophy, spirit and drive of an organisation have more to do with its relative achievement than do technology or economic resources, organisational structure, innovation and timing".

Sir Colin Marshall, moving from Avis to become chief executive of British Airways, undoubtedly believed that getting the culture right would be the key to success. In recent years this conviction has become more widely shared, to a large extent because so many analysts have attributed the high performance standards of much of Japanese industry to cultural factors which tie people together and give them purpose and meaning to their lives.

There are a number of issues to do with culture which are particularly relevant in the context of the talent-intensive organisation. If skills provide the cutting edge of competition, what management culture is wholly consistent with this belief?

Classifications of corporate culture

Typologies describing four main kinds of corporate culture have been put forward by Handy[4] in the UK and Harrison[5] in the USA. Handy's four types are as follows.

1 **The role culture.** This emphasises hierarchy, rules, procedures and structures, often referred to as bureaucracy.

2 **The task culture.** This emphasises achievement and is a team culture where objectives are a common factor uniting people.

3 **The cluster or person culture.** The individual is the focus and in as much as there is a structure it exists only to serve the individuals within it.

Such cultures are frequently found in professional partnerships such as firms of lawyers, architects or accountants.

4 **The power culture.** Rather like a spider's web, the power culture is dominated by the individual at the centre: the dominant chief execu-

tive or entrepreneur. In such a culture decisions reflect the distribution of power rather than logic or business needs.

Harrison's classification is similar. He uses the terms role culture, achievement culture, support culture and power culture. He goes on to make the point that in practice few corporate cultures are pure types but rather a blend of the four constituents. What distinguishes one company from another is the balance. Talent-intensive organisations need strong elements of achievement and support. They also need, however, some of the disciplines that go with the role culture and some of the drive and vision that derive from the image of a powerful leader.

Don Beattie, personnel director of ICL, was able to relate the development of the ICL corporate culture to this typology. Over the past few years the bureaucratic or role culture aspects had sharply declined while the achievement culture had moved strongly in the opposite direction. Although the element of support for the individual had "slipped a bit" it was still quite strong. There was little evidence of a power culture, since although the chief executive was charismatic and visionary he was also open, willing to be challenged and achieved consensus through the exercise of leadership skills rather than by pulling the levers of power.

In practice, however, managers do not often describe their organisations' cultures in such terms. The most common response to questions about culture is a list of adjectives or descriptive statements.

"It's a nice place to work, nice people to work with, there is pride in high standards of performance, in the intellectual challenge, we are proud of our history, we thrive on teamwork, we are proud of our integrity." (Kleinwort Benson)

"The culture reflects normal behaviour for the age group around; it's not seen as abnormal. Generally we have a young workforce who come to work dressed very individually. Corporate headquarters is very different from the operating companies. There is a lot of non-organisational type behaviour. There are outbursts and emotional displays, but when you look at what is going on, people are doing their jobs." (Unattributed response)

"It is a gentlemanly, conservative, stable, friendly, relaxed atmosphere, yet very successful. A very open company which understates its strengths. Looking after people well, professional with our clients." (Willis Corroon)

"I've never met any politics; people work together, they acknowledge the professionalism of their co-workers. There is a sense of comradeship but it can lead to introspection." (IBM, UK)

Sometimes the culture is described in terms of the key aspects of corporate life which symbolise or express it very clearly.

"Every year we have meetings in which we discuss this culture. . . generally in companies there are job descriptions, organisation charts but we don't have any of this . . . if you arrive at a meeting it is impossible to guess who is the boss . . . you can say what you like, even crazy things because it is often possible to find solutions from crazy ideas." (GSI, France)

In other cases a picture of corporate culture emerges in the form of a statement of "the way we do things around here".

"There is a culture here of doing things by consent. It's not possible for the top just to push things through without consensus. There's an element of personal co-operative management style. We don't use legal imperatives to push decisions. The idea will be spread first, there will be informal initiatives." (Bayer, Germany)

In some companies, notably Merck, the values were implicit and deliberately left unstated; in others, like GE-CGR, the values were developed as a result of a consultative exercise involving people from different parts of the company and different levels, and hence felt to be a general responsibility. Several respondents identified recent changes, sometimes in response to the needs of talent.

"The other shift has been from a muscle-driven organisation to a brain-driven organisation. We have now 10% graduates. . . . And all the assets as well as all the difficulties. For example, trying to bring talented people into a muscle-driven organisation when everything that you have in the way of rules, systems, regulations, is still keyed to the muscle-driven organisation. And the talents come and say: 'What is going on in this terrible set-up?'" (Continental)

The sub-cultures

Just as organisations need to employ different kinds of talent, so they need to accommodate different sub-cultures and to build bridges between them.

The main sub-cultures identified in the course of this study were as follows.

Managerial. The key values of this sub-culture are efficiency, profit, growth, competitiveness, quality and service. On balance managers lean towards tight controls, particularly financial controls, clear structures, formal systematic procedures, measurement and quantification, certainty and acceptance of authority. Managers like money, power, status and upward mobility through a career structure. They behave and dress soberly and conventionally.

The skills they respect include analytical ability, planning skills, numeracy, communication skills and decision-making skills.

Sales and marketing. The values in this group relate primarily to competitiveness, growth and individual achievement. There is less regard than among managers for formal procedures or tight financial controls, and little interest in quantitative analysis. In common with managers this group is motivated by money and status. They allow more scope for individuality in dress and behaviour. The skills they respect are those that make for the successful salesperson; in particular communications, negotiating and interpersonal skills.

Professional, technical and scientific. Although there are important differences between groups falling into this broad category – between accountants and architects, for example – there is one important factor that they share in common. Their values and attitudes are more determined by the profession or activity field they identify with than by the organisation which employs them. Thus scientists value truth, the free exchange of information, the scientific method. Money and position in the hierarchy are relatively unimportant, but the challenge of the job and a sense of achievement are vital.

The strengths and weaknesses of the various sub-cultures are summarised in Table 2.

Dominant, subsidiary and balanced cultures

It was clear that different organisations had developed cultures in which different sub-groups were the dominant ones in terms of having

Table 2   **Strengths and weaknesses of sub-cultures in talent-intensive organisations**

	Strengths	Weaknesses
Managerial sub-culture	1. Clear strategic direction 2. Focus on the bottom line 3. Strong systems and procedures	1. Inadequate understanding of core technology 2. Slowness to innovate 3. Failure to attract/retain/motivate top technical/professional talent
Marketing sub-culture	1. Focus on the market and the customer 2. Responsiveness to changes in demand 3. Responsiveness to competitor behaviour	1. Inadequate understanding of core technology 2. Failure to attract/retain/motivate top technical/professional talent 3. Weak financial controls (sometimes)
Technical/ Professional/ Scientific sub-culture	1. Leadership in technical innovation 2. Strongly motivated technical/professional employees	1. Lack of clear business strategy 2. Failure to focus on market/customer need 3. Failure to focus on the bottom line 4. Poor man-management (often)

influence on and exemplifying the company's values and also in terms of receiving the highest rewards and the chances of moving into the organisation's top jobs.

The managerial sub-culture appeared to be the dominant one in such companies as ABB and Philips in continental Europe, and Anspach Grossman Portugal and Baxter Healthcare in the USA.

The business-getting, marketing and sales culture is clearly strong in IBM and in Coley Porter Bell. ICL had a "technology-driven" culture in the past, but following the appointment of a new chairman and chief executive in the early 1980s a concerted effort was made to change to a "market-driven" culture.

The companies dominated by a scientific, professional or technical culture included GSI in France and SAS Institute in the USA. In *The 100 Best Companies to Work for in America*[6] it is said of Hewlett

Packard: "You may be handicapped here if you don't have a degree in electrical engineering."

On the other hand the UK-based computer consultancy AT&T Istel recruited a new director of advanced technology (head-hunted from ICL) following a decade during which the technological and creative side was "undervalued".

One or two companies, however, had developed something close to a balanced culture in which managerial, marketing and professional values were finding mutual understanding, mutual respect and the ability to work together in harmony. Hewlett Packard was striving for balance in its culture in a number of ways, including requiring all managers up to a fairly high level to be individual contributors (hybrids) and spend a significant amount of time on vocational work. "And in a sense, being just a manager in HP is not really acceptable in our culture."

Similarly, at SAS Institute: "Many managers try to keep their hand in on the technical areas, and this is true right up to the top of the organisation, including the president. We have no managers who are pure administrators." In Motorola the advantages of having a hybrid at the top were pointed out.

> "Now, we are in luck in that the very top guy is a technologist and a good business manager. George is a PhD in Applied Mathematics from Brown and was a Bell Labs research scientist for the first 14 years of his career before he joined us 17 years ago. . . . So he is able to recognise these issues when he does technology reviews and business reviews and when he walks around the plants."

The last section of this chapter examines two companies whose cultures are outstanding in their talent-nurturing properties.

CASE STUDIES

GSI

This is an example of a professional and scientific culture, task and achievement oriented. Now in its 21st year, the company employs 3,500 people.

Computer consultancy is its field of operations in which it is one of the largest European firms. It covers payroll, business, accounting and facilities management applications and is comparable with the three UK companies in this field that participated in the study – CMG, Data Logic and AT&T Istel – and the US computer consultancy SAS Institute.

The major elements of the culture are as follows.

- Decentralisation of decision-making.

   "Those companies where the decisions are taken by the chairman and so on, I think the company goes phut. What we want from people is that they help other people to solve problems not that they try to solve them themselves. That is why I do nothing.

   We use to help us the image of the nail and the hammer and we say that if I give you the nail – the responsibility – and I keep the hammer, then there is a big risk of some accidents. If I keep the power and you the responsibility I am sure that in time, maybe tomorrow, maybe in one month, you say keep your responsibility. Have it back, I don't want it because you hurt my fingers. And the real decentralisation is to give the hammer to the person who has the nail. Now everybody in GSI knows this image and every day we try to put it into practice."

- Helping people realise their potential. "What is talent and who is a talented person? Everybody. Everyone has talent. The only problem is to be sure that everybody can give you this talent so that you can use it." The main responsibility of each boss is to manage people.

- Lack of formal structures and procedures. "Generally in companies there are job descriptions, organisation charts but we don't have any of this. We are quite a flat pyramid." (This aspect of the culture is reinforced by presenting every new entrant with a copy of *Up the Organization* by Robert Townsend.)

- Lack of emphasis on hierarchy and status. "One of the things we enjoy is when people from the outside try to guess which is the office of the chairman because you can't tell." There are no distinctions between employees and managers.

- A rewards system which emphasises how individuals manage their people (do they encourage their education and training, do they develop them, and so on); the contribution of individuals to problem solving; and the support they give the boss. Salaries are determined on these criteria, never on results.

- The company is owned by its employees or at least by 1,400 of them, following a buy-out 4–5 years previously.

Hewlett Packard

Hewlett Packard (HP) is one of the world's leading electronics companies, a worldwide organisation making computers, calculators and a range of precision instruments and test equipment. Its head office is in Palo Alto, California, close to Stanford University. In 1991 its sales revenue was $14.5 billion and its profit before tax over $1 billion. It employs 89,000 people worldwide.

The company was founded in 1939 in the garage of Dave Packard and its first product was Bill Hewlett's audio oscillator. The business grew rapidly and was a $1 billion revenue-earner by the mid-1970s.

In 1957 Hewlett and Packard put their approach to running the business in writing in the form of a "Statement of Corporate Objectives". This has been reviewed and updated from time to time without undergoing radical change. Much of the philosophy is spelt out in an opening letter which states that if an organisation is to achieve its objectives it should strive to meet other fundamental requirements. These are, first, that the most capable people available should be selected for each assignment and that they should be given opportunity through programmes of continuing education and training. Second, that HP people contribute enthusiastically and share in the success that they make possible. Third, that all levels should work in unison towards common objectives. Fourth, in the context of clearly stated and agreed overall objectives, that people should be given the freedom to work towards those goals in their own ways.

The objectives, briefly summarised, are as follows.

- To achieve sufficient profit to finance company growth and provide the resources needed to achieve the other corporate objectives.
- To provide products and services of the greatest possible value to customers.
- To enter new fields only when we are sure that we can make a needed and profitable contribution.

- To let our growth be limited only by our profits and our ability to produce products that meet real customer needs.
- To help HP people share in the company's success.
- To foster initiative and creativity.
- To know our obligations to society.

The company's beliefs are set out in a document called *The HP Way*. Its central concepts are as follows.

- Belief in people; freedom.
- Respect and dignity; individual self-esteem.
- Recognition; sense of achievement; participation.
- Security; permanence; development of people.
- Insurance; personal worry protection.
- Share benefits and responsibility; help each other.
- Management by objectives (rather than by directive); decentralisation.
- Informality; first names; open communication.
- A chance to learn by making mistakes.
- Training and education; counselling.
- Performance and enthusiasm.

The company's human-resources policies and systems reflect this culture as well as being geared to the achievement of the corporate objectives. There is an "open-door" management policy ("management by wandering around"), few employee-management barriers, and recruitment primarily at the bottom, from college campuses. Selection tests are not used. A prime selection criteria is the assessment as to whether or not the individual will fit in with the HP culture.

Talent identification and placement in the early years is informal. At middle management level and above, managers are reviewed regularly and are assessed on technical, leadership and business skills. Appraisals are made in relation to objectives individuals have agreed with their managers. The rewards system is both demanding and egalitarian. It is also out in the open. HP makes extensive use of group recognition. Layoffs are to a large extent avoided by a combination of tactics including working overtime when business conditions are normal, taking pay cuts across the board in bad times, avoiding major one-off contracts, avoiding too much cyclical government business and maintaining a substantial direct labour sub-contract buffer.

HP has remained a highly successful business, with the culture largely intact.

"I still believe relative to our competition we are in better shape. We have some business fundamentals which are in better shape, we've never made a loss, we're self-financing, we've got no long-term debt. We are growing, we're going to grow. A bad year for us is growing at 10–12%. We used to grow at 18–20%. At the moment we're on something like 14% growth in the first quarter, but some parts of the company are still growing at 20%.

We have *The HP Way* which has phrases like uncompromising integrity, belief and trust in people, teamwork, and so on, but they are really strong cultural elements. We do things by consensus, we do things by personal interaction. If you ask someone to do something in HP, you expect them to tell you whether they can or can't do it straightaway, and you don't expect to have to chase people up . . . it would always be first names, no matter how high up or down the company you are; wherever you go in HP you would expect to start off a meeting with coffee. Coffee pots are very important. Wherever you go in HP people expect to be interrupted, managers expect to be interrupted, the job of a manager is to be interrupted. . . . There's a sense of treating other people in the company as a customer."

HP is given a glowing testimonial in *The 100 Best Companies to Work for in America*,[6] where it features in the top ten. The company continues to attract the top talent. In recent years, only IBM has recruited more MIT graduates.

SUMMARY

Within the broad objective of organisational effectiveness it is possible to identify five clear sub-goals which should guide the process of organisation design. These are as follows.

- Achieving an appropriate level of control.
- Achieving an adequate degree of co-ordination.
- Providing interfaces with key parts of the environment: customers, suppliers, and so on.
- Fostering commitment and motivation.
- Facilitating creativity and innovation.

These objectives are achieved by utilising three sets of "tools": structure; systems and procedures; and culture. The process of building an effective and enduring organisation is a process of social architecture. Given the objective of designing an organisation effective in business terms but also in attracting, retaining, nurturing and motivating highly talented people, respondents in the present study laid most emphasis on the role played by corporate culture, although there was some mention of structural factors.

In terms of structure the general view was that talented people respond best to one which is "flat" rather than hierarchical, which operates in a decentralised way with largely autonomous, relatively small sub-units.

Corporate culture is frequently defined as "the way things are done around here".

Charles Handy in the UK and Roger Harrison in the USA have developed similar typologies of corporate culture, identifying four basic types.

- The role culture: emphasising impersonal rules and procedures.
- The task or achievement culture: emphasising results.
- The cluster or person culture: emphasising the individual.
- The power culture: emphasising authority.

Successful talent-intensive organisations tend to have dominant cultures either of the task or achievement kind or (in the case of professional partnerships or consultancy firms) of the person or cluster kind.

In the course of the present study three main sub-cultures were identified.

- Managerial: emphasising efficiency, profit growth and competitiveness.
- Sales and marketing: emphasising competitiveness, growth and individual achievement.
- Professional and scientific: concerned with truth and information.

Each has strengths and weaknesses. In the talent-intensive organisations studied there was a tendency for one sub-culture to dominate the others.

References
1 Philip Sadler, *Designing Organisations*, London, Mercury Books, 1991.
2 Tom Peters and Nancy Austin, *A Passion for Excellence*, London, Macmillan, 1985.
3 Amin Rajan, *Capital People*, London, The Industrial Society Press, 1990.
4 Charles Handy, *Understanding Organisations*, Harmondsworth, Pelican Books, 1985.
5 Roger Harrison, *Organisational Culture and Quality of Service*, London, Association for Management Education and Development, 1987.
6 Robert Levering *et al.*, *The 100 Best Companies to Work for in America*, Reading Mass., Addison Wesley, 1984.

9

MANAGING HIGH POTENTIALS

Most large organisations attempt to identify, from among the pool of talented young people they recruit, those most likely to advance to top-level management positions, the "high potentials" ("HIPOs") or "high flyers". The process usually begins with two questions: what kind of business situation will they face, and what specific skills and attributes will they need?

A cross cultural study conducted by the Ashridge Management Research Group[1] of several UK and European companies showed how a number of major international enterprises were answering these questions. The main changes in the business environment identified in this study were as follows.

- An organisational context that is "flatter", faster-moving, market-driven, more cost-conscious, more fluid, more complex and much more challenging.
- An organisation that has more "surface" exposed to the external environment.
- An increasingly decentralised and fragmented organisation, yet one that is integrated by overall strategy and corporate culture (and probably, eventually, by information technology).
- The growing importance of "horizontal" management relative to "vertical" (that is, hierarchical) management (particularly caused by the need to manage issues such as quality, service and new technology "across" the organisation).
- An increasingly international environment that will include more diverse cultural groups.
- Unprecedented emphasis on people and talent as the organisation's most precious resources, on the need to utilise human resources fully and on the need to draw out people's commitment.

The last point is of particular significance in the context of the present study.

The different types of manager

What types of manager will be required to operate successfully at top level in such a changing context? Organisations involved in the Ashridge study were divided over whether they saw the need for one "ideal" type of manager or for a blend of different types. BMW, for example, took the view that the individual manager needs to possess three different kinds of competence (and, indeed, aims to gear its training and development activities to this model): a specialist, providing specialised expertise; an integrator, responsible for pulling the team together; and a *spielmacher* (gamesman) capable of recognising and using power within the organisation. BMW saw the relative importance of these three roles as shifting from specialist to gamesman as the manager moved up the organisation.

Specialists and generalists

Clearly, most organisations still attach fundamental importance to the need for specialist skills. At Electrolux, for example, the view was expressed that the manager of the future "must have specialist skills to give him (or her) status in the organisation". Shell UK's policy was that managers must have demonstrated "an ability to think in their own specialist area before adding on the relevant management disciplines".

At the same time, however, evidence from the study suggested that many managers will need to acquire general management skills at an earlier stage than in the past. ICL, for example, pointed out that the thrust of its management development policy was towards the development of greater general management ability (although it was emphasised that general management excellence should not be achieved at the expense of excellence in functional specialisations). The problem for organisations is to identify the specialists who will need those skills and to find effective ways of providing them.

Skills, knowledge and personal qualities

The profile of the senior manager of the future proposed by one of the companies indicated that he or she will need the ability to:

- relate to the economic, social and political environment;
- manage in a turbulent environment;
- manage within complex organisational structures;
- be innovative and initiate change;

- manage and utilise increasingly sophisticated information systems;
- manage people with widely different and changing values and expectations.

Other organisations give more direct emphasis to personal qualities, such as independence and openness to change, assertiveness, drive, tact or loyalty. This distinction, between knowledge and skills on the one hand and personality, attitudes and values on the other has been described by Cunningham[2] as the distinction between the "doing" and the "being" aspects of the manager's job.

The principal "doing" characteristics identified in the course of the Ashridge study were technical specialist skills, analytical skills and ability to think things through clearly, financial skills, and the other general management skills like marketing, planning and decision-making. All respondents, however, emphasised that "doing" is dependent upon people, and that a wide range of "people skills" will be required for management in the future, such as motivating, listening, counselling and delegating.

The "being" factors identified in the Ashridge study were "inherent" personal qualities and what might be termed the orientation or perspective of the individual. These qualities were listed at length.

- Bright and intellectually robust.
- Mentally agile.
- Enthusiastic and energetic.
- Resilient and tough; willing to cope with conflict.
- Confident.
- Strong willed and motivated to achieve.
- Committed.
- Honest with integrity.
- Flexible.
- Decisive.
- Open-minded and open to change.
- Creative and imaginative.
- Sensitive to other views and to "vibes".
- Desirous to "keep moving".
- Proactive and preventative in approach; not reactive and curative.
- Willing to take responsibility.
- Prepared to delegate and to live with it.
- Approachable and open-door.
- Business-minded and commercially aware.

- Able to take an integrated view of the organisation and understand the impact of his or her actions on the rest of it.
- Internationally aware and sensitive to other cultures.

Many of the managers interviewed emphasised that the doing skills outlined in the list above are not enough in themselves. Only when integrated with the being characteristics does the "whole" manager for the future emerge.

Characteristics of high flyers

What are the characteristics of existing high flyers? One interesting study of the origins and characteristics of 45 UK chief executives (Cox and Cooper[3]) found to start with that there was no class bias: 50% came from the middle class and 50% from the working class. There was "moderately strong evidence" that early self-sufficiency and responsibility is an important factor, often associated with loneliness or separation from parents. In addition there were some indications that parental expectations and encouragement play a part. (This is in accordance with the general research results reported in Chapter 2.)

They questioned the CEOs both about their motives and sources of satisfaction in work and about their values. The most frequently mentioned motives or sources of satisfaction were as follows.

- Intrinsic job interest.
- Achievement.
- Ambition.
- Determination.
- Developing the organisation.
- Working with people.
- Creative discontent.
- Power and influence.
- Independence.

Their most important values included the following.

- Family.
- People and relationships.
- Achievement.
- Independence.
- Initiative.

- Being yourself.
- Integrity.
- Perfection.

The research also elicited from the sample their views as to the behavioural or skill factors which they felt had contributed most to their career success. Those most often mentioned were analysis and problem-solving, skills with people, leadership, ability to learn from failure, risk-taking (described as moderate) and a high work rate. Personality factors were assessed using the Cattell 16 PF test (see Chapter 5, page 73). The scores of the sample were distributed very widely over most scales, pointing to the not very surprising conclusion that no one personality profile can be said to be typical of the successful senior executive. There was, however, a strong tendency towards being assertive, a tendency towards being outgoing and a slight tendency towards being emotionally stable, trusting, imaginative, experimenting, self-sufficient and shrewd.

Twenty-six of those taking part in the study took the KAI (Kirton Adaptor/Innovator) Test. All scored in the top half of the distribution, indicating that they are innovators rather than adaptors, and 54% came into the top 20% for the population as a whole, indicating that they are strong innovators.

Thirty took a Type A/Type B personality test developed by R.W. Borne. The concept was developed by Rosenman and his colleagues[4] during a study of patients with coronary heart disease. Type A people are competitive, high-achieving, aggressive, hasty, impatient and restless. They have "explosive speech patterns", tenseness of facial muscles and appear to be under time pressure. They are people so deeply involved in or committed to their work as to neglect other aspects of their lives. The results obtained with the 30 CEOs were highly significant. 57% were type A1, of which there are only 10% in the general population, and 90% either A1 or A2, compared with 50% in the population as a whole.

Cox and Cooper also reviewed a number of other studies from both the USA and the UK. The overall conclusions drawn from these as well as from their own work indicated that the following attributes characterised high flyers.

- Determination.
- Learning from adversity.
- Seizing chances when presented.

- Achievement orientation.
- Internal focus of control.
- Well-integrated values system: integrity, achievement, independence, initiative, people and relationships.
- Effective management of risk (moderate risk-takers).
- Clear objectives: personal and organisational.
- High dedication to the job.
- Intrinsic motivation.
- Well-organised life.
- Pragmatic approach (not intellectual).
- Sound analytical and problem-solving skills.
- High level of "people skills".
- High level of innovative ability.
- Type A personality.

In sum, success for this group was a function of philosophy (an emphasis on both task and people), skills (people and analytical) and motivation (characterised by a high need for power and strong intrinsic motivation).

Ensuring the future supply of top managerial talent

How is the organisation to ensure that it will have an adequate supply of potential top managers to meet its needs? Although the most common approach is to attempt the early identification of management potential by one method or another, by no means every organisation follows this approach.

Hewlett Packard is one of the few companies participating in the study not to have a formal high potential programme. The company's fundamental philosophy is as already described, to believe that people want to do a good job and that given clear objectives they should have the freedom and opportunity to go and find a way to do it.

The company faces an extremely rapid rate of change in its core technology. In 1991 50% of its revenue came from products less than two years old. Given the future uncertainties associated with such a pace of change the company is "not into long-term personnel planning like the oil companies have been, with their long-term succession planning and high-potential identification". Because the company is decentralised, the view is that each business will grow what it needs, "and if that's done within the context of a really strong HP culture, then you are going to have a very broad pool of talent from which you continuously keep choosing".

There are other companies with this view; Handy[5] quotes a leading US bank which states that it does not recruit "fast-track" people but that its training and development programme makes extraordinary performers out of ordinary people.

Baxter Healthcare previously targeted "high-potential" performers for prime developmental opportunities and actively monitored their development. However, the view was taken that although there were some advantages to this focused approach, the negative aspects outweighed them. These included what was referred to as "the Crown Prince Syndrome" and "implying that you either have 'it' to succeed or you do not. If you do not have 'it', your career is bleak". The new approach involves assessing individuals and developing each to their full potential. Baxter's current career development philosophy has put the responsibility for development with the employees and has sought to "empower them to manage their individual careers".

As part of the new approach the company has radically changed its assessment philosophy concerning individual potential. It has moved from a very evaluative approach to one focused more on development. Development reviews are conducted annually to assess an individual's skill set relative to current and future positions. Promotability ratings are assigned during these reviews to indicate timing of future moves, lateral or otherwise. For example, ratings may include "promotable in 1–3 years" or "develop in place" (meaning the individual is probably not going to move further towards the top of the organisation but will be developed in his or her existing job). The final category is for poor performers, in respect of which action is needed.

Currently there is less emphasis on ratings than in the past. In the course of the Employee Development Review (EDR) process, without assigning a rating or "putting a label on someone", a group of executives is able to meet and discuss, for example, a middle-level manager in his or her mid-30s who could handle a bigger job, but who has some significant development needs. This process can be carried out in an open forum, covering individuals at a particular level rather than concentrating on a smaller group of "high-potentials".

When should high flyers be identified?

One approach is to delay the identification of high flyers until the early "exploratory" stage of a person's career is complete and they have matured, developed a range of skills, and found out what type of work and work environment they are best suited to. On the other hand many organisations are attempting to identify their top managerial talent at an earlier age – even at the recruitment stage reflecting the fact that some people are now reaching top management jobs in their mid-30s rather than their middle to late 40s as was more common in the past. Clearly much depends on the growth rate of the business, how long it has been in existence and the age profile of the existing management.

Methods of identifying high potentials

A study of 70 European firms conducted in 1985[6] indicated that only three at that time were using assessment centre techniques to identify high potentials. Although the proportion is likely to have grown since then, not many of the firms interviewed for this book were using such a sophisticated approach.

Half the firms in the 1985 study were relying simply on nominations by line managers to some form of high-level review body which would make the final selection. In the current study most firms were using some form of systematic appraisal of potential, supplemented by the development of a wide range of opportunities for senior line managers and senior human-resources personnel to have face-to-face contact with those picked out in this way.

There was little evidence of the systematic use of psychometric testing and where it was used it appeared to play only a minor role in the decision-making process.

The development process

Given that the process of identifying potential for top jobs is reasonably validly carried out, how can that potential best be realised? What are the developmental processes which have proved most effective?

Research in this field has been ably summarised by McCauley[7] of the US Center for Creative Leadership. She has analysed the material under the headings of job assignments, other people and relationships, hardships and training.

Job assignments. On-the-job experiences are seen by managers as providing some of the most valuable learning experiences. For example, AT&T's Management Progress Study tracked a group of managers over 20 years. Initially 422 were put through a three and a half day assessment centre. There were two groups: recently hired college graduates taken on as management trainees; and non-graduates who had risen from non-management jobs. At the conclusion of the assessment process the assessors made predictions as to which would at least reach middle-management level.

Overall there was a significant relationship between the predictions and the level achieved. However, the results showed the strong influence of the amount of challenge in the job as rated by the managers themselves. For example, among the college graduates who were predicted to fail but who also experienced challenging work 61% actually reached top management. Of those who were predicted to succeed, but who experienced low job challenge, only 30% made it to middle management.

The possibility of self-fulfilling prophecies must be acknowledged, however, since those perceived as having high potential will tend to get the most challenging assignments.

Other people and relationships. The research evidence on the influence of these factors does not point to clear conclusions. Nevertheless mentoring and coaching are used by many organisations as developmental processes. Even if the boss does not act as coach or mentor the individual's relationship with his or her boss can have a powerful impact on development. The behaviour of the boss serves as a model, whether positive or negative.

There is evidence to the effect that those who get to the top have wider networks of horizontal relationships than others. In a study carried out by Kram and Isabella in 1985 and reported by McCauley, managers in one corporation were interviewed and invited to identify relationships with peers that they felt had helped develop their careers. The developmental processes most often mentioned were:

- information sharing, both for technical knowledge and organisational perspective;
- career strategy sharing, helping each other learn about career options; and
- feedback, helping each other learn about strengths and weaknesses.

Hardships and training. Managers often experience business failures, mistakes, dismissal and other setbacks. A crisis of this kind can provoke introspection, analysis of the individual's strengths and weaknesses and consequent efforts to improve or change direction.

As to training, the critical issue is not so much whether training results in learning as whether or not the learning gets transferred to the job. Top level executives do not tend to place strong emphasis on the part played by formal training in their own development.

Chapter 10 looks at the approach taken to developing high flyers by seven of the companies interviewed for this book.

What happens when it goes wrong: executive derailment

Researchers at the Center for Creative Leadership have made a particular study of the process of "executive derailment", defined as occurring when a manager who was expected to go higher in the organisation, and who was assessed as having the ability to do so, is dismissed, demoted or "plateaued".

In one early study[8] 19 top-level executives who had taken part in action to "derail" a high flyer were asked to give their reasons. These included both personal quality issues such as insensitivity to others, arrogance or betrayal of trust, and managerial shortcomings such as failure to delegate or inability to think strategically. Other studies confirmed these findings and also suggested other reasons such as narrowness of business experience, poor image, lack of disciplined judgment and lack of in-depth knowledge of the business.

Further questions were suggested by these findings. Could the reasons for derailment be reduced to some basic clusters of flaws or defects? Are some flaws more likely than others to be damaging to a manager's career? Would the same flaws necessarily harm career prospects in different companies with different cultures? What is the relationship between flaws and managerial skills? Are certain flaws more likely than others to affect a manager's ability to handle particular jobs? Are derailed and successful managers viewed differently before derailment takes place?

Further investigation did indeed identify six specific clusters of flaws.

- Problems with personal relationships.
- Difficulty in moulding staff.
- Difficulty in making strategic transitions.
- Lack of follow-through.
- Overdependence, or staying in the same field too long.
- Inability to handle differences with management.

The last was the least significant. Difficulty in moulding staff and in making strategic transitions were significantly related to derailment in six of the eight companies studied, however, while lack of follow-through was also important.

A parallel study, the CCL research programme "Benchmarks",[9] showed that in general flaws were most strongly related to the ability to handle the most challenging and complex jobs, and least related to the ability to handle functional job rotations.

Managers having difficulty with relationships were seen as not being able to handle assignments calling for powers of persuasion or the need to develop new working relationships.

It also asked whether derailed and successful managers are viewed differently in advance. The finding here is of considerable importance. It is that derailment can be predicted in advance. A combination of factors, if identified in time, can together point to problems ahead. These are:

- lack of "hard" management skills such as strategic thinking or the ability to follow through; and
- lack of certain personal qualities such as flexibility and tolerance of ambiguity, coupled with moving into challenging jobs which expose flaws.

The importance of this conclusion is clear. Derailment wastes talent. It not only wastes an organisation's investment in the past development of the individual concerned, it also frequently involves personal distress.

One way to prevent or at least reduce the incidence of derailment is to improve understanding of the requirements for real success in higher level jobs and to improve the ability of the organisation both to assess and to develop the competencies, skills or attributes that match these requirements.

Other important steps that can be taken, none of which is capable of being reduced to a simple formula or technique, are to:

- create an environment where learning is taken seriously;
- provide support and counselling when managers reach the critical transition points in their jobs; and
- plan career development so as to avoid "late surprises".

Perhaps most important is to create a culture in which individuals who realistically perceive the extent of their management strengths and are aware of their limitations can nevertheless enjoy recognition for the value they do contribute to the organisation and do not have to feel that they have failed if they rule themselves out of eligibility for the very top jobs.

Developing the international manager

In the increasingly global context of business the search is on for a new form of rare managerial talent: the individual who is able to operate successfully across different national cultures.

Philips, for example, holds that tomorrow's executives will need "to be truly international. This implies not only knowledge of different parts of the world, different cultures, political and economic systems, but also genuine acceptance of the differences and an empathy for people motivated by different values."

Managers who operate away from their country of origin need all the qualities expected of a top managerial performer and more. At the top level they have to be competent in handling governmental relations; they need particularly strong financial management skills in view of the importance of transactions across the foreign exchanges; above all they need to be able to handle major socio-political issues such as environmental conservation or co-determination and worker participation.

An Ashridge Management College[10] survey invited companies to nominate the five most important characteristics required of the international managers in their organisation; see Table 3.

Table 3 **The most important characteristics of international managers** (%)

Strategic awareness	71
Adaptability in new situations	67
Sensitivity to different cultures	60
Ability to work in international teams	56
Language skills	46
Understanding international marketing	46
Relationship skills	40
International negotiation skills	38
Self-reliance	27
High task-orientation	19
Open, non-judgmental personality	19
Understanding international finance	13
Awareness of own cultural background	2

Individual companies emphasised particular characteristics. Rhône-Poulenc stressed that its managers must think "world" not "France". General Electric looked for a vital quality that James Baughman, GE's corporate management development manager, refers to as a "global brain": the ability to comprehend world trends as they affect the business, to understand competitors on a global scale, and to appreciate the world standard of competition that is required to be a winner. Baughman believes that among the qualities that predispose a person to a global outlook, the most important are curiosity and openness.

From the Ashridge survey it emerged that companies regard direct personal international experience at an early age as the most effective method of developing international skills and perspectives. When companies were asked, however, how many of their managers currently have such experience the general indication was that the proportion was low, in the region of 10–15%, although significantly greater among high flyers. In most companies the need to increase the number was seen as an important objective.

International career planning at its most sophisticated is to be seen in highly international companies such as Unilever, the Anglo-Dutch foods-to-detergents enterprise. At any one time this company has around 1,000 managers working outside their home country. An average spell overseas lasts four years and by the time people reach the top levels of the business they will not only have worked in different countries, but also in business units comprising mixed nationalities. Unilever describes its approach as "short-term succession planning but long-term talent planning".

Young managers of high potential can expect a process of career development that will move them both between countries and across functions. They can expect early responsibility for producing results and to have their experience supplemented by formal training. Every job is seen simultaneously as something that needs doing and as a developmental opportunity.

Issues and problems in the management of high potential

The current study, together with previous research in this area, has identified a number of commonly encountered issues and problems.

- Those identified as having high potential are given the most challenging job assignments and are the most favoured in terms of other developmental opportunities, particularly the most expensive and prestigious forms of external formal training. This gives rise to the issue of the self-fulfilling prophecy.

- Those not so identified – and particularly those who marginally fail to be included in the high potential category – may become resentful and lose motivation accordingly.
- If those of high potential are promoted too rapidly they may not stay in any one job long enough, either for the purpose of learning and developing or from the viewpoint of the need to evaluate their performance.
- There is the danger that local national or divisional chief executives will try to hang on to their brightest and best people rather than contribute them to the overall company pool of talent.
- The increasing expectation that future top managers in international business must have had international experience creates a requirement of international mobility which is not always easy to fulfil.

  One reason is that many of the young persons concerned, whether male or female, will have spouses who have their own careers to follow and who only exceptionally will be able to synchronise their postings to coincide. Another, which applies in the main to somewhat older personnel, is the question of children's education.
- Expectations can be created which are then difficult or even impossible to fulfil. This point was often made during the present study which was conducted in the context of a global recession and particularly severe economic conditions in the USA and the UK. Companies were contracting in size, qualified personnel at all levels were being declared redundant or offered early retirement options and in most cases graduate recruitment, if not suspended altogether, had been savagely cut back. Not unnaturally in such circumstances, individuals begin to question the extent to which promises of exceptional career progress can be honoured.
- Young people on the high potential list are often put under considerable pressure to compete and to provide superior performance. This can lead to a form of "burn-out", a physical or emotional response to the stress of the situation which will call for extremely careful and sensitive handling if it is not to lead to the loss of a valuable individual. It has been suggested that it is the most highly talented of all who are the most likely to experience this problem.
- Several companies were alert to the danger of not providing similarly attractive career development opportunities for outstanding technical or professional people. One answer is to pay more atten-

tion to the development of alternative career paths for such people, the so-called dual career ladder.

The dual career ladder

The development of dual career ladders reflects some assumptions based on experience in many settings. The first is that most technical, scientific and professional specialists look for the recognition, standing and rewards that go with advancement or promotion through a hierarchical system of grades or ranks. The second is that only a few of such individuals wish to become managers. Often they accept managerial positions because other routes for advancement do not exist.

Those who do opt for a managerial career often make poor managers. In the words of a French respondent in the present study: "It is not possible to love both people and technique."

There is some research evidence which relates to these assumptions. In a study reported by Allen and Ketz[11] 20% of engineering students at MIT quoted management as their ultimate career goal. They also surveyed over 2,000 scientific and technical personnel in nine organisations. Of 2,157 respondents, 1,495 expressed a clear preference for a particular career path. The managerial ladder was preferred by 33% and the technical ladder by 22%. The largest group, however, amounting to 46% of the total, chose a third option: "the opportunity to engage in those challenging and exciting research activities and projects in which they were most interested, irrespective of promotion".

It was also found that preferences varied with age and that as engineers grew older they were even more likely to choose the third option.

These results, however, conflict with findings reported by Garden[12] who studied the career aspirations of software developers in 11 high-technology companies. Here the largest group, 34%, expressed a preference for a managerial career. The proportion preferring a technical ladder was 24%. A further 24% chose a fourth option: to start up their own business. Finally, only 15% wanted a series of challenging projects rather than to be upwardly mobile.

The differences may well reflect differences in age and in the particular organisation cultures. Nor can it be assumed that the different options are equally attractive from one company to another. Both these studies were conducted in the USA and Allen and Ketz assert that in most US companies the prestige goes with the manager's job. Vice-president as a title carries much more status than a title such as senior research fellow. In the UK too scientists, engineers and technicians have traditionally enjoyed lower status than generalists. In France and

Germany, however, where engineers, particularly, enjoy a very high standing in the community, it is more likely that the status conferred by a high position on a technical ladder would prove satisfying.

Much does depend, of course, on the care and attention paid to the development of alternative career paths and to ensuring that the rewards, both tangible and intangible, associated with them are as attractive as those associated with the traditional managerial pyramid. At Dow Corning a dual ladder system was found to lack credibility, due to lack of top management commitment and the use of the technical ladder as a "dumping ground" for failed managers. The company took a fresh look at the problem,[13] believing that it was essential to recognise and encourage technical knowledge and creativity. It now has a managerial ladder starting at Grade V and going up to Grade VIII, and three professional ladders starting at Grade I and rising to Grade VIII. These are research scientist, development scientist and process engineering scientist.

SUMMARY

Most large organisations attempt to identify those most likely to get to the top positions, the "high potentials" or "high flyers". A common starting point is to take a view about the future situation top managers will have to face and from this scenario to draw some conclusions about the attributes, skills and knowledge that will be needed. In some cases the emphasis is placed on requisite knowledge and skills, in others personal qualities and orientations are seen as most important.

Research studies of yesterday's high flyers, people who made it to the top, show that successful achievers in management do possess some common qualities and attributes. They tend to be powerful personalities, assertive, outgoing and emotionally stable. They are frequently trusting, imaginative and experimenting. They also display self-confidence and self-sufficiency. They are original, with a low tendency to conform. They are also hard-driving, aggressive and heavily involved in their work.

It is frequently the case that they have had early unhappy experiences, setbacks or deprivations and that they have learned from adversity, being more determined and more achievement-oriented than most. They have well-integrated values systems and value integrity, people and relationships as well as achievement. Formal management education has not been relevant; much more significance is attached to early work experience and in particular the opportunity to hold real responsibility at an early age.

Not all companies try to identify their "high flyers" at an early stage in their careers. Those that do rely in the main on nominations by line managers in the context either of a system for appraising both performance and potential or one which focuses solely on proven performance. A minority of companies uses assessment centre techniques.

The most effective processes used to develop high flyers include challenging job assignments, mentoring, coaching and "sponsorship" by senior executives, learning by working with particular bosses (positive and negative role models), relationships with peers, hardships and setbacks.

Not all high flyers actually make it to the top. Studies of those who are "derailed" en route have identified six major types of flaw associated with "plateauing". These are problems with interpersonal relationships; difficulty in moulding staff; difficulty in making strategic transitions; failure to follow through; overdependence; and strategic differences with management.

Many companies are paying particular attention to the "quest for the international manager", a future manager who will need not only knowledge of different countries, different cultures and different political and economic systems, but also genuine acceptance of such differences and empathy for people holding different values. Others are concerned with developing dual career ladders designed to satisfy the aspirations of both specialists and generalists.

References

1 Ashridge Management Research Group, *Management for the Future*, Berkhamsted, 1988.
2 Ian Cunningham, "Patterns of Managing for the Future", Paper presented to the conference "Positioning Managers for the Future", Ashridge Management College, 1987.
3 Charles J. Cox and Cary L. Cooper, *High Flyers*, Oxford, Basil Blackwell, 1988.
4 R.H. Rosenman, M. Friedman and R. Strauss, "CHD in the Western collaborative group study", *Journal of the American Medical Association*, vol. 195, pp. 85–92, 1966.
5 Laurence Handy, "Managing the high flier", *Employment Gazette*, June 1987.
6 C. Brooklyn Derr, "Managing High Potentials in Europe: Some Cross-Cultural Findings", *European Management Journal*, vol. 5, no. 2, 1987.
7 Cynthia McCauley, *Development Experiences in Managerial Work: A Literature Review*, Technical Report 26, Greensboro N.C., Center for Creative Leadership, 1986.
8 Michael M. Lombardo and Cynthia D. McCauley, *The Dynamics of Executive Derailment*, Technical Report 34, Greensboro N.C., Center for Creative Leadership, 1988.

9 Michael M. Lombardo, Esther Hutchinson and T. Dan Pryor, *Benchmarks*, Greensboro N.C., Center for Creative Leadership, 1989.

10 Kevin Barham, *The International Manager*, The Economist Books/Business Books, London, 1991.

11 Thomas J. Allen and Ralph Ketz, "Managing Engineers and Scientists: Some New Perspectives", in Paul Evans *et al.* (eds), *Human Resource Management in International Firms*, Macmillan, London, 1989.

12 Anna Marie Garden, "Career orientations of software developers in high-tech. companies", *R&D Management*, vol. 20, no. 4, 1990.

13 Charles W. Lentz, "Dual ladders become multiple ladders at Dow Corning", *Research Technology Management*, vol. 33, no. 3, May–June 1990.

10

SEVEN COMPANIES' APPROACHES TO THE DEVELOPMENT OF HIGH FLYERS

Of the 50 companies interviewed for this book, seven have been chosen as case histories for this chapter. They illustrate the range of different approaches currently taken in order to identify and develop high flyers around the world.

CASE STUDIES

Asea Brown Boveri

Asea Brown Boveri (ABB) is a group with 1,300 companies operating in 120 countries. Its director of corporate staff management resources, Arne Olsson, defines high flyers as people in the 30–35 age bracket who are candidates for a major company president job. He stresses the need to identify management talent "early", which in the ABB case is around 30 years of age. The typical individual in this company will be a university trained engineer, who has been in the firm for 3–6 years.

> "At that age you can get a sense of whether they have something. You speak to his peers, you find out about the person. If you interview a large number of 30 year-olds you will be able to say these four or six I have to find out more about. You have a sense based on experience that there is something extra to these people."

It is considered that good preparation for taking charge of a company of, say, 1,500 people at around age 40 is to run a division of that company, or a similar but much smaller company, for the preceding three years or so. The preparation for such a job in its turn could be to act as a functional manager, a role to be taken up around age 34, and the typical preparation for that would be some such post as production planning manager, starting at 30–31. This, in the ABB view, is why talent must be identified early, since development, which is seen in terms of learning on the job, takes time.

Some will fail, some will leave, others will reach a plateau. Through a constant process of discussion with their managers their development is monitored. There is no attempt to have a uniform, group-wide system for performance appraisal and succession planning, however, with standard forms which are sent back to the centre. The approach used in a particular company or country is a matter for the local human-resources director.

> "I just want to know, in say a company of 10,000 people, a ranking of the people on the level below the president of the company, perhaps a group of 7–8 people. In most of these companies I know these people or have met them. I want to know how they are being ranked in terms of performance and, above all, potential for future assignments internally and externally. I also want to know who are the possible successors to that level; say about another 20 people."

Taking the Swedish group of companies as an example, which employs about 30,000 people, there are about 45 who might benefit from exposure to other companies and who might be candidates for the very top level. At the next level there are some 200 candidates for running smaller companies in the size range 300–700 employees. At the third level there are a similar number in the high-potential group, those who are judged to have extraordinary potential for higher level jobs. This gives a total of 400–500 people that the local headquarters concerned is keeping track of, with a similar number in other countries.

Arne Olsson lays great stress on the importance of line managers getting to know potential candidates personally. "Line managers are the real personnel managers." The ABB group has "very tight staffing". One person is employed in human-resource work at the centre where companies of similar size and international scope often have several. The philosophy is strongly anti-bureaucratic. "If there is one thing that line managers hate it is if they have to do a lot of reporting."

There is considerable emphasis on matching people to positions and on taking into account the context of the position and the culture, the ways of working. Olsson perceives differences between what he terms the "givers" and the "receivers". Givers are managers who produce good people; they attract them, train and develop them, expose them to challenges and help them to grow. If there are three companies in a group, when there is a discussion of potential candidates for a job it is often the same company – the giver – that produces the candidates.

The givers attract people over the long run since it becomes known that that company grows people. "The person running that company might suffer a short-term problem with a guy moving out and on but it pays off in the long term for him because his company is like flypaper for the good people." That is the real challenge: how to make people feel they belong to the group as a whole and to act in its long-term best interests. The support from the very top was seen as of critical importance.

> "Maybe the most important thing you have – or not – is the kind of signals that are coming from the very top of the company; what I call the carbon-paper effect, the effect on the whole company of the behaviour and values, and so on, of the people at the top as guardians of company attitudes . . . . If the president of the company says 'This issue of talent is important my friends, you have to work with this and spend time on it, and I will review with you every year or so what is happening out there', then this is a very powerful signal . . . . If the top person in the company says 'This is very important, we should really do more about this, now sorry I have to go because I have an important meeting and just carry on', that is to send a contradictory signal."

Bayer

Bayer does not regard talent as a stable commodity, but something that can be developed from a basis of excellence. The company also emphasises social skills, however, and looks for people with that extra, special experience that goes beyond the basic qualification; involvement in student or youth activities, travel, language ability, for example.

There are about 5,600 people at management level in the company. Of these roughly 2,000 are chemists, 1,000 engineers, 1,000 "merchant people" (marketing), about 200 each of physicists, biologists and pharmacists, 100 mathematicians and about 60 lawyers.

Chemists mostly begin their careers in the laboratory. Each individual receives 2–4 weeks' training a year for three years after entry.

> "All of these professionals have to learn to lead people and manage the

various businesses. In the first few years there is a lot of training directed towards these objectives and also the first tests to see if they can lead people and can see the business sense behind their work. They attend one- or two-week courses which are given by company personnel. The subjects include communication, leadership, presentation skills, accounting, planning, labour laws, environmental protection laws, introductions to business administration and marketing."

There is a contrast between this broad approach and that which is more common in the USA and UK, more often tailored to individual needs and preparing individuals for particular jobs. "We want to give someone such a wide background and range of skills that later it is possible for him or her to fill a number of different jobs."

There are regular performance reviews — once a year for the first five years — at which individuals will be told what level they can expect to reach, and what career their manager thinks they are capable of. There are guide-lines and recommendations as to how the performance review should be carried out but there is no laid down structure as to how it must be done. The practice began ten years ago and took some time to gain acceptance, but now the right to a performance review is generally exercised.

Another issue is cross-function mobility.

"Years ago we had what we in Germany call 'chimney careers'; you started in one department and you retired from the same department . . . now we have extremely high internal mobility . . . cross-functional from one department to another. So we have opened up a lot of opportunities, naturally, and also a lot of uncertainty . . . so obviously there are questions from people as to where they will be in 3–5 years' time, and we have to find some answers to these questions."

This has meant opening a company-wide labour market. There is a proce-dure for keeping track of those with high potential. Lists are kept and dis-cussed at various levels and the top layer is discussed by the board several times a year. The word "potentials" has become part of the German lan-guage. There are four committees, the sole purpose of which is to discuss management development for those with high potential, one each for engi-neering, production, marketing and sales, and administration. Above these is a committee for senior executives and general management.

People are picked out in the period beginning about three years after entry and continuing until they are about 45 years of age. In the functional areas the average age for the "big lists" is 35–40. For the executive and general management area there are two layers. One, very small in number, consists of those who are seen as capable of moving to the very top levels and the average age is 45–47. The larger group, not necessarily destined for the very top, has an average age of about 43. There is a check or control on the work of these committees through the succession planning that is done for all senior management positions. In relation to these jobs, departments are asked to nominate people who sooner or later could be promoted to fill them. The resulting names are then compared with the "potentials" lists and if there are people who appear on the one but not on the other, questions are raised.

The total number of potentials make up about 10–15% of the management-level staff of the group as a whole.

Solvay

Solvay is the principal manufacturing company in Belgium and a world leader in the chemical industry with some 45,000 employees worldwide. The company is well known in Belgium and is able to be very selective in its recruiting.

During the first 3–5 years graduate entrants are given various tasks through which the company finds out which are "specialist-minded" and which are "management-minded". The policy is to give them challenging tasks immediately on joining to test and develop them. If they respond they may be sent abroad to widen their experience both functionally and geographically. At the very least they will move to a new position within Belgium. A willingness to be transferred is essential.

The respective line managers in the various divisions and subsidiaries abroad are responsible for the career development of their staff. They train them, follow them up and evaluate them; they are expected to carry out regular appraisals for both performance and potential.

Yearly remuneration is mainly based on the individual's assessed potential. Performance is rewarded by a lump sum bonus, but potential is rewarded by an increase in the monthly salary. This system has been in use for over 20 years.

The aim is systematically and periodically to follow up each individual case, although the number of people whose potential has to be evaluated is very high. For example, is the potential of a person who was evaluated five years ago confirmed today or not? The company is now considering using a computerised information system to improve its approach. Such a system would enable the company to target a certain group of people and to list potential candidates for the jobs to be filled. It is essential to maintain regular contact with foreign subsidiaries for this purpose in order to provide the centre with accurate, up-to-date information.

In Solvay decision-making is largely delegated to the divisions and subsidiaries. When the centre sees the need to move someone from a plant to fill a middle-management vacancy the human-resources function tries to convince the line management concerned to release the individual. If the answer is no, the decision is respected. The human-resources function will, however, point out the need for management development and that the way a manager manages people shows how well that individual is doing his or her job.

Executives know that there is a department in Brussels dealing specifically with career development and when they visit the centre they try to find time for a discussion. If individuals feel that they are not fully occupied or are looking for a move they should first take this up with their local management. If that does not work they know there is someone at the centre they can talk to.

There is a wide range of career development programmes. Internal development seminars focus on personal development and there are specific courses on motivating people and communications. The high potentials are sent to business schools, regardless of their seniority. The Young Executives Programme, attended by about 120 people a year, is a week-long course which conveys information about the company and reinforces its culture. There is also a Seminar for Executives at senior level which has been running for about 23 years and draws people from all over the world.

Solvay lays considerable emphasis on the notion that "individuals are the main actors in their career development".

Philips

Philips is one of the world's major electronics companies, employing 240,000 people worldwide. There is a process of formal management development review both for the product divisions and for the large national organisations. At least once a year the human-resource function meets divisional presidents to review key positions, succession planning and the pool of young people of high potential. The group involved in these discussions is made up of the company president, the president of the relevant product division, the human-resources director, the managing director of the Corporate Staff Bureau and one or two other key executives. Following the review meeting an action plan is drawn up which it is up to the division concerned to implement. There is a Corporate Potential Appraisal System which identifies a number of personality characteristics which by experience have been shown to be predictive and valid for future career success. (The validity studies were carried out some time previously by a qualified psychologist and updated more recently to take account of changed circumstances, including changed views of what comprises relevant managerial behaviour.)

The average age at which young potentials are identified for the first time is 28–30, usually about five years after joining.

There are three main approaches to development:

- getting to know the business through challenging assignments;
- career paths with planned job rotation; and
- formal management training.

At some point in the career of a young potential who could possibly grow to be a general management type there should be international experience. Management development, including succession planning, is seen as a line management responsibility. "The HR specialist is a catalyst in the process. He or she can even be very pro-active in it but it is not their final responsibility."

Formal management training is available at various stages. Some takes place in the national organisation; typically business orientation training focusing on the issues in that organisation. Some is provided by product divisions and some at corporate level. There is, for example, an International Management Course for those in their 30s, and an International Programme for Senior Executives for people at that level regardless of age (anything from 35 to 55). For younger people there is the "Octagon", a taskforce type of training for younger talent. People around the age of 34, after one week of formal training, are given an assignment in which they can interview anyone in Europe and subsequently produce a written report for the board that is also to be presented. The assignment lasts for about three months, but it has to be done without giving up the individual's current job. There are three octagons a year each involving eight people. This is a European initiative but there are similar development opportunities in the USA.

As well as the regular appraisal system (which is operated with varying degrees of effectiveness in different countries) the company is currently introducing a corporate-level approach career document for the group that is considered key from a corporate point of view (about 200 people in the key posts to which the board makes appointments), the potential successors to these (another 600 people) and the pool of top young potentials (a further 1,000 or so). This is termed the "corporate interest group".

Line management commitment is seen as vitally important. Line managers' contribution is in the process of being built into the appraisal system.

> "Not least because last year for the first time the president has agreed, together with me, to conduct the Management Development Reviews. That's going to have a very big effect. So the culture and the mentality of the company is changing in that respect."

L'Oréal

L'Oréal is one of the most international companies based in France. It is a world leader in cosmetics and has an important pharmaceuticals division. Entrants begin as trainees and for the first few weeks learn about the company: what the products are; how they are made; how they are marketed and sold. "In L'Oréal you always begin at the bottom – even if you have a PhD – and then you climb."

Initially people have performance reviews several times a year, but after 2–3 years they are done annually. This provides an opportunity for the individual to ask for training and development or career moves. The director-general of human resources travels frequently to keep in touch with overseas companies, where he meets local boards, middle managers and young managers with high potential.

> "When I go to a company I am thinking: do they have good quality people for the future? That is my obsession: to raise an international management of top quality. We want to find these people and push for them to realise their potential. The CEO has said that we want people to be colonels at 30 and generals at 35."

L'Oréal is a participant in CEDEP at Fontainebleau. Linked to INSEAD, CEDEP provides development programmes for a consortium of companies of which there are 22 at present. People at the level of marketing director or the head of a laboratory are sent there about six times in two years for two weeks at a time.

> "We also have a centre to run conferences on cultural subjects: music, painting, and so forth. We think it good for people who think they have no time to spend a weekend there. Ten or twelve people will get together, they will talk with a famous pianist or someone will talk about particular paintings. It's good for our people and for us because it opens people up and broadens their outlook.
>
> We identify our high potential people through watching them working. For instance if someone has outstanding results that will not necessarily mean that he or she is one of the brightest people in the company. We might even be more interested in the way a person will behave and run a very tough business with a lot of difficulties . . . . It is important that people have had experience of bad difficulties and problems, of failure."

The best training is believed to be on the job. L'Oréal people do learn through seminars, but mainly through meetings and seeing how other people work.

> "In marketing, for example, we don't have the situation where young product managers will only work with their group product manager . . . they will be round the table with their group product director, with the marketing director, with the managing director of the department, and at least once a month with the vice-president of the division they belong to, so that they will have hundreds of cases and examples of marketing experience. And that is the way you will learn at L'Oréal. Everyone at that meeting will behave as equals."

Another important principle for high flyers is the "right to fail". The L'Oréal definition is that they should be creative and ambitious, that is, prepared to take risks.

> "If you want risk-takers they must know that they won't be in trouble if they fail. Of course you can't fail every time; then we'll know there is a problem. But all of us will have difficulties at first and we make mistakes or things happen in the economy or the environment that you cannot predict. Nothing is certain, which makes our job exciting. At L'Oréal we have fun, it's hard work too but we enjoy it here. This is part of our culture."

Colgate Palmolive

Colgate Palmolive employs 27,000 people altogether. Its human-resource planning systems are at present bottom-up, from subsidiaries cascading up to division and corporate level. At the corporate level staff are primarily concerned with the top three levels of management, as well as with exceptionally talented people. The people described as having high potential are hence a very small proportion of the total. They are mainly managers and professionals who have already opted for regional or global career paths.

The planning process uses a very simple grid (see Figure 4) based on individual profiles of those in the management group as well as some below them, detailing their strengths, their development needs, their potential short-term job moves and their long-term potential. Typically, reviews and judgments begin with the individual's line manager but extend to those made by the management of a particular subsidiary group. It is considered important to get a cross-functional view of people, rather than just a single function view. The division presidents review the top line appraisals by each subsidiary management group during their personal visits. Eventually this gets pushed up to corporate level.

The individual ratings arise from annual appraisals, the executive incentive programme results, and so on. This gives the performance trend (horizontal axis). On the potential side (vertical axis) potential for leadership, broad business knowledge and financial judgment, strategic insight, teamwork, and development of others are assessed. Functional excellence is assumed for both sides.

- **A** potential essentially means that the individual can become a strategic leader; typically a corporate role, a vice-president level job.

Figure 4 **The Colgate Palmolive grid**

	A	B	C
A			
B			
C			

- **B** potential is general manager, maybe moving from a small to a larger subsidiary.
- **C** is current level in the organisation.

A consolidated worldwide grid is constructed for people in certain job categories at various levels. For example, a grid of general managers might include the worldwide population of about 65 people at present. Doing this shows up those people who are not going to move beyond their current job (who are, for example, close to retirement) but are "high performers". "These are the places where we should be putting the younger 'A' potential marketing people, who are the young tigers needing a real challenge and a really good coach."

A very healthy group of people is identified occupying the middle positions on the grid, performing well and able to grow within that general manager category.

There is also a good number of people in the upper left hand section, with "A" class potential and "A/B" class performance over the long term: achieving or overachieving their individual objectives, and having the business knowledge, teamwork and other qualities to give high potential.

The challenge is in making the judgment, even using the specific criteria that have been described, to ensure that the right people move into senior management. The leadership skills that are required of senior management are different from the excellent management skills that are required lower down. The distinguishing features include the ability to develop and articulate strategy and to gain commitment from others, and leadership skills to manage the execution of strategy (as opposed to the execution of current tasks). So a whole set of factors called Strategic Leadership Skills has been developed.

"Looking at our current high-potentials (particularly in the marketing function) we have many people with BA degrees as well as with MBAs. So not all of our high potentials are MBAs. And we do not encourage current employees to go and get MBAs, unlike some other organisations which might send people on executive MBA programmes or whatever. We tend to say, if you do that, do it for self-enrichment to build up your capacity as a learner. But we do help with the fees if people wish to do further study in their own time, for example. We would not support a BA who wanted to go off and do a full-time MBA though. We do use executive level development for people much further down the line in their particular careers."

National Westminster Bank

This leading UK financial institution recruits as potential managers both graduates and school leavers (18 year-olds with A level qualifications). Over the years the proportion of graduates is rising as fewer able students decide to start their working careers at 18. The bank has also become more amenable to post-experience recruiting, taking recent graduates with work experience as well as some entrants directly into middle management in their mid-30s, including some MBAs. The company view is that following the current recession the resurgence of demand for young talent combined with demographic trends will lead to shortages and that a further shift in emphasis to post-experience recruiting may well be necessary.

At this initial stage the bank looks for a cross-section of young people of varying ability and potential and offers a wide range of starting salaries, with higher rates (assistant manager level) for post-experience entrants. The aim is, however, to include within this range a few potential high flyers each year. The vast mass of the graduate recruits are described as "good, upper second-class honours degrees, recruited for their personal qualities, able to handle customers as well as operate systems".

The selection procedure for graduates uses the assessment centre method. There are, in fact, three distinct streams.

- The A scheme consists of the high flyers who will start on an assistant manager's pay and who will normally have a relevant degree in banking or finance. Some will have been sponsored by the bank on appropriate degree courses at Bangor or Loughborough universities; there are 12 such sponsorships annually. This group also includes some post-experience entrants. A scheme entrants normally commence their careers in London.
- The B scheme consists of the mainstream graduate entrants who could have studied almost any subject. These could start at a major regional centre of the bank as well as in London.
- The C scheme consists of those who start at local branches of the bank. A lot of the entrants are happy to start in this way in their own locality. The pressure on them to succeed is not so strong. Nevertheless there have been some remarkable career successes in this category.

There are flexible training arrangements covering the first two working years. "The target is to bring graduate management trainees into line with other, non-graduate trainees by about age 24. After that we aren't very interested in their educational background." At the age of 24 they embark upon the more formal parts of the management development programme. There is considerable reliance on the use of assessment centres and the preparation of personal learning programmes. The objective is to learn by their late 20s who are the real high flyers.

Following an initial assessment centre experience in their early 20s the candidates attend a one-week Career Development Centre in their middle to late 20s. This results in each individual being allocated a trained mentor as his or her personal development adviser to facilitate the achievement of the Personal Development Plan.

Identified high flyers go through a further programme known as an Executive Development Workshop. This concentrates on general management competencies.

The company makes considerable use of psychometric tests in its selection and assessment procedures, including tests of verbal and numerical reasoning, the Myers Briggs Type Indicator and the Kirton Adaptation/Innovation test which measures capacity for innovation.

The use of tests has a long history in the bank and some of those tested originally now have 20 years' service so that it would be possible to carry out some validation studies. "It is tempting to get into pure research like a university." But there are other priorities. There is confidence in the validity of a combination of exercises and tests, as used in the assessment centres, as predictors of performance over the ensuing five year period. Examination of people's performance once they get to senior levels shows that it cannot necessarily be predicted from their past performance at more junior levels. Some get into difficulty when promoted beyond a certain level. The common failings lie in the areas of analysing information, leadership, presentation skills and personal impact.

Trained line managers act as assessors at the career development centres. These are "not too senior", in other words not so old that they are out of touch with the age-group. They tend to be drawn from those in lower-middle management with high potential themselves. They are particularly trained in the art of giving feedback. A typical assessment centre would involve two parallel streams of 12 candidates with three assessors for each.

High flyers attend external management development programmes on a reasonably regular basis. UK centres such as Ashridge, Cranfield or Henley are used, as well as INSEAD and IMD in Europe and a number of US business schools including Harvard, MIT, Wharton, Virginia, Columbia, Carnegie-Mellon, Northwestern and Amos Tuck. Attendance on these programmes is funded by the centre.

The current approach is to encourage people to seek continuous learning and be more pro-active in identifying their training needs.

Use of competencies

The bank began to employ a competency-based approach to job selection five years ago.

Profiles of jobs are compared with profiles of individuals. "We have been digging the foundations for this for five years. There is an awful lot still to be done. It is relatively easy to do the job profiles, much more difficult to do the personal profiles." Performance assessment data need to be converted into a personal profile based on the same competencies as the job profile "but redesigning the appraisal form doesn't transform the average reporting officer into a skilled competency assessor".

An example of the use of the new approach is the way corporate account-executive jobs are filled. In the past "good people" were assigned to these jobs, but they were not always good at what was needed in this type of role. Competency analysis established the key factors for success and an appropriate selection process was introduced.

In respect of the processes by which performance is influenced the company uses a standard performance appraisal system. Increasingly senior managers see themselves as having an important role to play in development and bringing the best out of people, although there are still too many who do not see this as part of the job. The main emphasis, however, is placed on self-development, based on the personal development programmes which result from the assessment centres.

National Westminster is a member of a consortium of companies, including BP, Coopers & Lybrand, British Telecom and the North Thames Regional Health Authority, which supports a "tailored" MBA programme. Six or seven candidates are sponsored for this annually plus six or so on part-time MBA courses. It remains to be seen whether these people are at or near the top in 10–20 years' time.

National Westminster has compared its approach with that of other leading companies including BP, Shell and Philips. "We are satisfied that we are well up with the leading organisations in the field of management development, but there is still plenty to do."

11

PLACING A VALUE ON TALENT

How much value do companies place on their top talent? This question can be answered in three ways. The first is by looking to see what the company says about its value and contribution to the success of the organisation. The second is by examining company practice for evidence that talented people are, indeed, treated as valuable assets. The third approach is to attempt to express the value of talent in financial terms, including some form of human-asset accounting.

Statements which indicate that talent is valued

Several of the annual reports made available by companies taking part in this study make reference to the important part played by people, particularly the most talented, in achieving company goals.

- GSI, referring to the setting up of GSI university, states that this "completes the array of tools GSI uses to cultivate its main value, the quality of GSI women and men, at the service of the client".
- Merck attributes its success largely to people – "more than anything else, our people have earned great respect for Merck, across America and around the world" – and mentions its continued drive "to recruit scientists of the highest calibre". The chairman and chief officer's report to stockholders closes with this tribute to the company's employees. "Exceptional in their skill, their energy and their dedication; they are in my opinion an unstoppable force working to benefit society and to ensure an outstanding future for our company."
- Marsh and McLennan, in its shareholder letter, makes the point that it "concentrates on providing the right environment to attract and motivate outstanding professionals" and in the final paragraph goes on to acknowledge that "our growth would not be possible without the dedication, commitment and expertise of Marsh and McLennan companies' 24,000 employees around the world."
- CMG's report carries a section headed "CMG people" which emphas-

ises the efforts put into "the search for high quality people" and quotes a past chairman: "Our rate of growth is limited only by our ability to recruit suitable personnel."

- Rockwell's report for 1991 makes the basic point that "the knowledge of its people determines a nation's standard of living and a company's global competitiveness". A drive for continuous improvement – what it describes as Leadership Performance – is said to tap the full potential of Rockwell's people; their skills, knowledge, creativity and driving desire to be the best.
- Data Logic states that it is the quality of its people which has distinguished the company as a leader in its market sectors.
- Bayer in its 1990 report has a section on people which refers to the importance of motivation and professional enthusiasm, carefully targeted recruiting and continuing education.
- British Airways' report for 1989–90 also has a two-page feature entitled "A team dedicated to being the best", written by the director of human resources, in which it is acknowledged that it is the contribution of people which gives BA its competitive edge.
- The value placed on employees generally by IBM (UK) is evidenced by the considerable space devoted to reporting aspects of their involvement in the company in the annual report, including details of international assignments, notable examples of the suggestion programme's success, the investment made in further education, the results of opinion surveys and progress in the field of equal opportunity. Very unusually, IBM (UK)'s report mentions individual employees below director level by name.

It does not necessarily follow, of course, that statements like these reflect actual company practice in the way they treat talented people. Nor does a failure to acknowledge the role of talented people in the annual report indicate that the company does not value them highly. One US company, working at the leading edge of technology and utterly dependent upon the dedication and creativity of exceptionally talented people, published an annual report in 1990 which read as if the corporation were a black box into which money is poured at one end and world-class breakthroughs in technology emerge at the other. There is no mention of people at all – apart from the names of the directors and officers – just products, money and markets. Nevertheless this company goes to great lengths to avoid layoffs of scientists, provides paid sabbatical leave after seven years' service and in other ways demonstrates that it places considerable value on its creative researchers and technologists.

Actions which demonstrate that talent is highly valued

If companies really do see talented people as the most important form of investment for the future they will tend to do all or most of the following things.

- Senior line management, often including the chief executive officer, will be directly and regularly involved in such activities as recruiting, acting as assessors at assessment centres, as mentors for young persons with high potential and as tutors on formal management development programmes. Among the many companies in the present study which meet this criterion are British Airways, IBM (UK), ICL, Prudential Financial Services, Merck and Philips.
- There will be a "no layoffs" policy or at least a policy of resorting to layoffs only as a desperate last resort. This is explicitly part of corporate policy at Hewlett Packard, IBM and Intel, among others.
- The company will invest substantially in continuing education, training and development. This is the case in the majority of companies studied. Several, such as Glaxo, GSI, IBM and Motorola, have their own university-standard education centres.
- There will exist processes for the maintenance and nurturing of talented people suffering from stress, mid-life crisis or burn-out. These include employee assistance programmes, internal counselling services and sabbatical leave. Companies such as IBM, Xerox and Glaxo have such processes in place.
- The company will have positive policies to ensure that rich sources of talent are not overlooked because of discrimination on the grounds of sex, race or religion. No company which consistently ignores the potential talent existing in the female population, for example, can be validly described as one which truly places a high value on talent. US companies tend to lead the way here through "affirmative action" programmes; Xerox, IBM, Corning, Merck and Baxter Healthcare all provide good models.

Placing a financial value on talent

The value human society places on talent in purely financial terms is established through market mechanisms in a variety of ways. The prices paid at auction for works by great artists, the fees commanded by world-class performing artists, sports men and women, entertainers, consultant surgeons, lawyers, architects, fashion designers, and so on, or the transfer fees paid for star players in the European soccer leagues, are paralleled in business organisations by:

- the salaries and related benefits paid to internationally mobile top-level business executives;
- the value of stock options companies are prepared to allocate to key personnel;
- the earnings of "super salesmen" (often higher than the earnings of their own chief executives);
- the extent to which a company's market capitalisation falls when one or more highly talented employees leave;
- the fees companies are prepared to pay to search consultants in order to hunt down the most talented to fill particular vacancies;
- the sums companies are prepared to invest in graduate recruitment programmes, selection procedures, management development programmes, and so on.

There are many more examples, but the point has been made that it is not too difficult to arrive at a monetary value for talent. It is generally known what top people in their various fields are approximately worth in the context of the values system of society.

The reflection of value in salaries and benefits

The most direct and tangible answer to the question "What is the value of talent?" is to be found in what companies are prepared to pay in order to attract, retain and motivate the best people. In this sense there is a "market" for talent and one that is becoming increasingly international, particularly in respect of top-level general managers and world-class professionals, scientists and technologists.

The companies involved in the present study virtually all monitor the "going rate" for various categories of talent, from college graduates through to chief executives and Nobel prize-winners, although those on the European side of the Atlantic are perhaps not always fully aware of how much higher total compensation packages can be for key personnel in the USA.

The "going rate", however, can be a misleading indicator of the true value of talent since in most instances the bargaining power of huge corporate employers of talent will greatly outweigh that of talented individuals, particularly those being recruited for their potential rather than their track record of achievement. (Collective bargaining in the context of exceptionally talented people is virtually non-existent.) A much more accurate picture of the true financial worth of a particular type of talent is created when the talented person stands outside the organisation and sells his or her services in the role of entrepreneur rather than employee. This is an increasingly frequent practice in such fields as business consulting, IT consulting, insurance broking and investment counselling.

What Tom Peters was paid in salary when a McKinsey consultant is not known, but his daily rate would certainly have been a small fraction of the fee he can command for one of his well-known personal appearances before hundreds or even thousands of top-level business people.

It is also frequently the case that certain kinds of talented people – research scientists in the pharmaceutical field for instance – have no notion of what the value of their talent is in financial terms, nor, in many cases, are they particularly interested in finding out.

The UK press recently carried yet another "brain drain" story of top scientists leaving the UK for the USA, in this case the entire research team at St Mary's Hospital Medical School in London which had made a breakthrough in finding a specific genetic cause of Alzheimer's disease. The team had been headhunted by the University of Southern Florida, which offered them significantly higher salaries as well as better facilities than those they were enjoying in the UK. The new salaries were not disclosed, but if the researchers instead of responding to the University of Florida's offer had issued a glossy brochure describing their research and their qualifications and had circulated it to the world's leading universities and pharmaceutical companies, including those in Japan, they would almost certainly have been able to achieve significantly better terms. This may well be the form that the "brain drain" takes in the future.

The lesson for companies is to look beyond prevailing market rates for talent and to take a view about the real underlying value to the business of its talented people, particularly those few really exceptional people, whether in management or in specialist roles, on whom the future prosperity of the organisation largely rests.

Such an approach was exemplified by the thinking of one UK chief executive, referring to a key employee, the sales director, whose basic salary was £97,000: "This has been checked out externally with search consultants. It's about right, but I have put him up to £115,000 because I believe he is adding value to the business. If he moved our sales figures could drop 15–20%."

Valuing people as assets

There have been very few attempts outside the academic world to develop human-asset accounting. This is the process of placing a financial value on an organisation's human assets and endeavouring to use such information for various purposes such as valuing a company for acquisition or merger purposes, calculating how efficiently human resources are being used, or carrying out a cost-benefit analysis in respect of particular human-resource strategies. Although in recent years the accountancy profession has become more flexible in its approach to the valuation of intangible assets, progress has been confined largely to those such as brands, patents, copyrights, licences and goodwill which have an advantage over human assets in that they cannot just get up and walk away.

Nevertheless there is a strong argument for initiatives to take greater account of human assets. The world's stockmarkets react to a series of familiar financial indicators of a company's health such as return on capital employed, earnings per share, level of borrowing and reserves. Dependence exclusively on such indicators can, however, be misleading in respect of talent-intensive industries, particularly in the case of the prospects for long-term investment. In such cases there is a need for information about the intellectual or talent "capital" of a business and the competence and foresight with which it is being managed. Current conventional financial indices can, indeed, be grossly misleading if they conceal a failure to invest in the maintenance and future supply of human talent.

One example in recent times of the potentially misleading nature of profitability and return on capital as the main yardstick for knowledge-based companies has been the UK-based pharmaceuticals-horticulture group Fisons. This company achieved a remarkable growth record throughout the 1980s, with high profitability fuelled largely by success in the world's largest market for ethical pharmaceuticals, the USA. The development of novel drug delivery systems and new formulations during that decade provided shrewd patent extensions and enabled the company to capitalise on a basic research breakthrough of the 1970s. Most of the company's revenues were generated by a single chemical entity developed in that period known as sodium cromoglycate, which formed the basis of its numerous medications for asthma and seasonal allergies. No other major breakthroughs have been achieved since.

To secure a long-term competitive advantage in the talent-intensive pharmaceutical industry requires serious levels of investment in the intellectual capital of basic research and development, and in the continued development of novel manufacturing technologies. Throughout the 1980s Fisons significantly underfunded these vital elements of its business. The result is that the company's R&D pipeline in the early 1990s is looking seriously deficient as a means of securing future revenue flows beyond the expiry of its current drug patents, and its manufacturing technology has been publicly criticised as no longer being up to the standards for the industry.

Fisons's R&D expenditure for 1990 was £68.9m, representing 5.6% of group turnover. If the entire amount was spent in the pharmaceuticals division and none at all allocated to the larger scientific equipment division, which is highly unlikely, then the investment in R&D would have amounted to 13.8% of turnover. In 1989 the figures were 4.6% and 9.7% respectively. R&D spend as a percentage of sales in other major European pharmaceutical manufacturers is typically higher: 14% in Glaxo, 1990/91, over 15% in Bayer.

Share values plunged in late 1991, when the Nikko analyst commented: "Investors have been badly let down in that the company underplayed the seriousness of its problem."[1] In January 1992 the chairman and chief executive resigned abruptly "on grounds of ill health". Share values recovered at this news, but his departure was followed by more disturbing information. US documents released under the Freedom of Information Act showed that UK production of a new asthma drug, Tilade, had been breaking US regulations. Share values fell back as the company publicly acknowledged that its manufacturing processes had not always been "as tight as they could have been".

Human assets are mobile

The accountant's view of an asset is something of value that can be represented as a credit item on a balance sheet. Capital assets are fixed assets and, although they cannot be readily converted into cash, they are tangible and can be quantified in monetary terms.

Quantifying intangible assets is more difficult, since these comprise such characteristics as goodwill, patent rights, copyrights and similar elements of a business that have no physical substance. The active debate in the late 1980s concerning the valuation of brands is a good example of the practical issues that can arise. During that decade, a wave of aggressive acquisitions highlighted major disparities between the value of a company as represented in its standard company accounts and the value put on it by takeover bids. The differences often arose from the possession of major global brands. These were highly significant intangible assets, which frequently reflected substantial marketing investments over many years. They conferred earnings potentials that were inadequately reflected by traditional accounting procedures.

Lloyd[2] has described this particular problem in forthright terms: "The valuation anomalies indicate a systematic failure on the part of auditors in their duty to shareholders to render an accurate record of the company's net worth." There would seem to be a very real risk that, during the 1990s, the increasing contribution of intellectual capital and human talent will be similarly undervalued by company auditors and senior managers, who cling to inappropriate economic models of the firm.

In the knowledge-based companies of the 1990s and beyond, the land-labour-capital model of production is becoming an anachronism. It is no longer appropriate to treat workers simply as an expense item on the profit and loss account. The contribution of such human talent is becoming the crucial means of gaining and sustaining competitive advantage and, as such, is no longer a cost item to be minimised. As this book has sought to illustrate, companies such as Merck, Hewlett Packard and ICL are ahead of the throng in recognising that significant revenue flows can only be maintained by tomorrow's products or services. Firms which are competing on this basis need to invest in attracting and nurturing the key human talent. The fact that human talent is mobile, and that its formal "ownership" by a company is not possible, is the very reason why knowledge-based companies need to pay more attention to investing in, attracting and retaining key staff.

Accounting for human resources

During the 1960s and 1970s professors and academics at leading US and European business schools addressed themselves extensively to the subject of accounting for human resources. In practice, the output of many of these research activities was high in statistical theory but relatively low in accessibility and practical, managerial application. No attempt will be made here to revisit those complex issues, other than to address some of the essential concepts. Certainly none of the companies taking part in the present study was making any serious attempt to engage in human-asset accounting.

Traditional attempts to put a value on human resources have tended to take an historical cost-based approach; that is, seeking to measure the organisation's investment in human resources. For example, in 1967 the R.G. Barry Corporation of Columbus, Ohio, introduced human-resource accounting in its annual report. The company worked out costs for each manager under five headings, namely: recruiting, acquisition, formal training, informal familiarisation, and experience and development. The costs were then amortised over the expected working lives of the individuals and unamortised costs (such as when an individual left the company) were written off.

An alternative approach is to try to measure the replacement cost; that is, the cost of recruiting, selection, compensation and training costs. This updates the valuation but is equally (or more) subjective.

The example of the professional soccer player has already been mentioned. The value of such a player is reflected in his market value on the European transfer market. It has been suggested[3] that, by analogy, where a company had several divisions seeking the same employee, he or she should be allocated to the highest bidder and the price incorporated into that division's capital base.

Another approach is the expense model which focuses on attaching monetary value to the behavioural outcomes of working in an organisation, costing such things as labour turnover, absenteeism and job performance. In this approach there is at least some attempt to address the output side of the equation, although in most organisations few methods exist for quantifying such variables.

The so-called utility analysis[4] is a method that can be used to assess factors influencing job performance. It therefore has application in the valuation of human resources from an output perspective. This method takes a statistical approach based on the expectation that the variation in outputs from a large number of people, carrying out essentially the same job, will follow a normal distribution. The particular distribution is defined by the mean ± the standard deviation. Recruitment and selection methods might be designed to ensure that only the most talented are selected, those defined, for example, as the top 15% performance band. In practice, this approximates to a job performance level that is one standard deviation above the mean (that is, around the 85th percentile).

In terms of the monetary value of human job performance, the practical application of the utility analysis has given rise to a rough rule of thumb: that one standard deviation in performance is approximately equal to 40% of annual wages for that particular job function.

From such data Smith and colleagues[5] have argued that the development of rigorous selection procedures is one of the most cost-effective investments an organisation can make. They cite Schmidt and colleagues who, in 1979, calculated that by using a simple pencil-and-paper aptitude test to select computer programmers, the US government (which then hired about 618 new programmers annually) could save up to $97m.

The extent to which these output-based methods of valuation can be applied to professional knowledge-workers is debatable, although there is perhaps a case to be made for investing in attempts to do so. Using a financial asset model as a starting point, the two analogous dimensions for investments in human talent would be current performance and future potential. These are akin to the earnings contribution and price appreciation, or growth, of the more traditional investments.

Value added

As implied by the foregoing discussion, an important measure of the performance of talent of intellectual capital is value added. The value of a product or service is created by two basic resources: the skill, time effort and know-how of employees; and the use of working and fixed assets. Both involve costs. People have to be paid and tangible assets have to be bought and depreciated. These costs are the first claims on created value. What is left after pay and depreciation are extracted is operating profit and, after interest and tax, earnings per share (EPS). However, because added value is the source of profit, it is a better guide to company performance than EPS. Value added shows how productive people are before taking into account their costs.

In a service organisation in which professional staff are directly involved in revenue generating activities, the value added by particular individuals or groups is relatively easy to quantify. This is especially true in firms providing professional services (such as firms of management consultants, accountants, solicitors) which are able to bill clients in direct relation to the time spent on particular projects. So, calculating fee-generating capacity is a simple arithmetical exercise. Under these circumstances, even junior staff are usually billed out at levels appropriate to their cost base. A general rule of thumb for many jobs in such professional service organisations is to double (or treble) the labour costs as a charge to the client. (In the case of trainee staff, there may be the temptation to suppose that an individual's contribution to value added will be negative during the first 2–3 years of employment. However, this is generally too simplistic. The future earnings potential of such talent will be high, and the use of relatively simple accounting techniques can demonstrate the net present value of such individuals. Demographic data and demand forecasting with respect to particular technical expertise or know-how can also inform the process of calculating net present value and the likely earnings potential of junior staff.)

The value added by talented individuals to the businesses of other types of talent-based firms can be considerably more difficult to quantify. Nevertheless, some rough estimates can be attempted. For example, at the level of a particular operational sub-unit or business unit, it may be possible to gauge the relative proportion of total value added, and then to compare this with the average costs incurred.

In the case of a pure R&D function (traditionally viewed as an internally generated expenditure and written off in the year in which it is incurred) it may be more appropriate to take an historical view of value added. The products of previous research endeavours will often be seen in intellectual property, such as patents, trademarks and copyrights. These enjoy property rights (that is, ownership can be established and protected in law, and the assets can be bought and sold). Accountancy conventions allow such intellectual property to be quantified on the balance sheet. Thus a view can be taken of the value added by previous R&D activities to the present business situation, and extrapolations made.

More difficult to quantify, but potentially of greater significance, is the degree to which research and development adds to the organisation's core competencies at the level of human skills and experience; that is, the enrichment of the intellectual asset base. This book has already highlighted excellent examples, in the corporate cultures of Hewlett Packard and Merck; arguably, Xerox and Intel might also come into this category.

The value added to a business by other elements of the firm's value chain might best be estimated from market-research data. Ultimately, the value added to a product or service is dependent upon the price the consumer or client is prepared to pay. So a better understanding of the buying decision is likely to provide insight into the value adding process, and allow a rough estimate to be made of particular functional inputs to that process. Beyond that, the relative contribution of particular individuals might be crudely estimated, at least by their immediate line manager.

A study carried out by Lloyd[6] assessed the dependence of quoted UK investment banks on their staff, in terms of their contribution to the market value of their respective organisations. In an article published in *Financial Weekly* in October 1987 he produced the following table (Table 4).

The data reveal an interesting contrast between the order of companies ranked according to market value and according to their people-dependent assets. Clearly, at the time of this analysis, the relative value

Table 4 **UK banking staff and market value**

Company	Market value £m	Net assets £m	PDA[a] £m	PDA ratio	Staff no.	PDA per head £'000
SG Warburg	862	506	356	0.41	2,164	164.5
Morgan Grenfell	818	371	447	0.55	2,675	167.1
Hill Samuel	630	194	436	0.69	5,212	83.7
Hambros	560	251	309	0.55	4,118	75.0
Kleinwort Benson	530	365	165	0.31	2,402	68.7
Schroders	402	177	225	0.56	1,030	218.4
Guinness Peat	334	159	175	0.52	1,045	167.5
Henry Ansbacher	136	54	82	0.60	319	257.1
Brown Shipley	85	44	41	0.48	733	55.9
Averages				0.52		139.8

[a]PDA (people-dependent assets) = market value – net assets.

added to the businesses by the human know-how assets of Henry Ansbacher and Schroders was significantly higher than those, say, of Brown Shipley and Kleinwort Benson.

Salaries tend to consume the largest part of the added value in traditional industries, but in knowledge-based companies the salary share may be a significantly smaller fraction of the added value. Lloyd estimates that in more traditional manufacturing companies staff costs can account for as much as 70% of the value added, whereas in knowledge-based businesses (such as merchant banking and securities trading) this figure may fall to as low as 10% of the value added. He has suggested that value added per £ of pay is set to become one of the key measures of talent-intensive businesses over the next few years. He has calculated, for example, that by the late 1980s every 1p increase in value added per £ paid in salaries by the principal UK telecommunications company BT was worth another £21m at the level of operating profit.

However, an appropriate balance will always need to be reached in terms of the salary share of staff as a fraction of the total value added, particularly in knowledge-based companies which employ highly experienced and talented individuals. It has been said that the skills and intellect of such individuals are never fully "for hire", and the risk of mobility of human assets has already been mentioned. Talented knowledge-workers may or may not have the entrepreneurial spirit to establish a business of their own, but given their own particular abilities to add value to a business, this is always a factor to be borne in mind. It therefore follows that the salary share is likely to provide a good indicator of how vulnerable a knowledge-based company is to the sudden loss of key staff.

CASE STUDY

Cergus

Sveiby and Lloyd[7] describe the case of Cergus, a subsidiary of the Swedish information company Argus, established in 1980. During its early years it was successful in a buoyant Swedish market that was hungry for advice on mergers and financial strategy. The firm extended its activities into merchant banking in 1982, when a third party took a majority stake, and by the second full year as a broking firm Cergus was earning SKr50m (£5m) and employing over 60 people.

However, a 50% acquisition of the Cergus parent company took place in the second half of 1984, without the knowledge of senior Cergus managers. During the angry reactions which followed, the remaining (two) founder members of Cergus were fired. When the pair joined a competitor firm many of their professional team at Cergus followed them, and over a relatively short period of time some 25 senior staff left. This resulted in a £10m loss of market value of the parent group when the Swedish stock exchange finally became aware of the haemorrhage of senior, revenue-generating professionals from Cergus. It has been estimated that the value of Cergus per se was more than halved within a month.

SUMMARY

In the final analysis, it is unlikely that sophisticated financial analyses will be applied routinely to the valuation of human talent. However, companies are depending increasingly on their intellectual capital to continue to compete in today's markets, and investment in this vital resource requires a clear appreciation of its significance and a forward-looking assessment of the worth of individuals. It is no longer good enough for companies to issue superficial statements like "our people are our greatest asset" and yet continue to regard know-how expenditure as a cost item to be minimised. Although the quantification of human talent in monetary terms is often exceedingly difficult, this cannot and should not deter those in positions of strategic leadership from securing at least a semi-quantitative view. Value added per £ of pay is one measure which looks likely to become more widely used.

References

1 *Daily Mail*, December 31st 1991.
2 Tom Lloyd, *The Nice Company*, London, Bloomsbury, 1990.
3 J.S. Hekimian and C.H. Jones, "Put people on your balance sheet", *Harvard Business Review*, vol. 45, pp. 107–113, January–February 1967.
4 H.E. Brogden, "When testing pays off", *Personnel Psychology*, vol. 2, pp. 171–183, 1949.
5 M. Smith, M. Gregg and R. Andrews, *Selection and Assessment – a New Appraisal*, London, Pitman, 1989.
6 Tom Lloyd, *op. cit.*
7 K.E. Sveiby and T. Lloyd, *Managing Knowhow: Add Value by Valuing Creativity*, Bloomsbury, 1987.

12

THE STRATEGIC MANAGEMENT
OF TALENT

The key to the successful strategic management of talent is the realisation by top management that, in the talent-intensive organisation, business strategy and human-resources strategy are inseparable.

The City of London study

This has seldom been so clearly stated as in a study carried out in 1990 by personnel directors and managers from institutions in the UK financial services industry, mostly in the City of London and members of the London Human Resources Group. They looked at the City's likely requirement for highly skilled people in the period to 1995 and beyond, and at the strategies needed to recruit, train and retain them.[1]

The study was prompted by growing recognition of the fact that in the increasingly competitive field of international financial services, the key factor in achieving competitive advantage is people, and that institutions needed to develop business and personnel practices which treated them as a capital asset generating profits. The rapid proliferation of new financial instruments, coupled with new technology means that the City no longer prospers by buying and selling money; its chief source of income is derived from the buying and selling of expertise.

The City of London has in 1 square mile the biggest concentration of talent in any area of similar size in the UK, equalled only by the financial districts of New York and Tokyo. Talented people in scarce supply account for over half the City's workforce and over three-quarters of its future staff requirements. They are needed, and competed for, by seven main industries: banking, other credit-granting institutions, securities dealings, insurance, accountancy and management consultancy, legal services and software services. The study had four specific objectives.

- To identify future skill requirements of these seven key industries.
- To identify critical competencies required by the talented personnel.
- To identify ways of acquiring these competencies.

- To identify the various challenges posed by the task of managing such workers and to suggest ways of meeting them so as to improve overall standards of human-resource management.

Analysis of the business situation and likely future trends in each sector built up a picture of the future requirements of the City as a whole for talented personnel. (Although the deep and lasting recession in the UK economy since the report was published would no doubt result in a downward revision of requirements in terms of sheer numbers, the points concerned with the quality of the workforce have gained added emphasis in the context of significantly heightened competition.)

It was concluded that all the industries, with the exception of securities dealing, would require an increase in the percentage of staff with higher education qualifications and appropriate intellectual skills. Out of an estimated 46,000 additional employees needed by 1995, 36,000 would fall into the high-talent category. The bulk of the increase would be in software services, legal services, and accountancy and management consultancy.

The research team found that there were some constraints preventing the human-resource function from being fully effective, including the following.

- Lack of clear corporate strategies providing direction and coherence to training and development.
- Financial pressures.
- Perceived unimportance of the human-resource function.
- Lack of adequate human-resource planning.

Until about 1988 a traditional view of personnel prevailed among senior City executives, who gave low priority to human-resource issues. The sheer speed and scale of change had given rise to a short-term, firefighting response, and there was a widespread absence of systematic procedures in areas such as recruitment, appraisal, training and promotion, as well as a general lack of business and planning skills among human-resource staff.

The penalties for neglect of a strategic approach in the mid-1980s were uncontrolled growth in staff costs, the emergence of practices such as "golden hellos" and "golden handcuffs" which severely distorted salary structures, cultural "black holes" when people from different firms were brought together in an environment in which the old paternalism had disappeared but nothing had been put in its place, and a tendency for individualism, self-interest and greed to triumph over group identity and loyalty.

Problems included wholesale defections of entire teams to competitors, inability to convert training into greater job effectiveness and blockages in internal communication.

The report concluded that each City institution needed to ensure that its corporate culture had at least two features.

- Motivational. Open, communicative, supportive, establishing a clear mutuality of interest between the institution and its staff.
- Integrative. Integrating all functions within it so as to achieve an overall effectiveness greater than the sum of the parts.

Some German, Japanese and Scandinavian institutions operating in the City had created such cultures. Their staff retention rates were relatively high and they were experiencing few recruitment difficulties.

Strategic management issues

The key issues in the strategic management of talent highlighted by this study include the following.

- The extent to which top management in the talent-intensive organisation recognises and grasps the implications of the fact that talented people are the key assets and the chief source of lasting competitive advantage.
- The extent to which, in consequence, human-resource strategies are seen as central to business strategy.
- The extent to which, in consequence, human-resources specialists are fully involved in the preparation and implementation of strategic plans for the business.
- The extent to which top management, and in particular the chief executive, see human-resources issues as those to which they should give priority, both in terms of the allocation of finance and their own personal time and effort.

In talent-intensive companies business strategy and human-resources strategy are inseparable. It is not a question of what contribution human-resources specialists can make to the formulation and implementation of a "business" strategy, conceived as something separate from the human side of the business, and to do with the use of a range of analytical tools and a combination of marketing and financial expertise. It is rather that the long-term success of the business in attracting, retaining, developing, motivating and utilising the best talent in its field is likely to be the biggest single factor in determining its long-term commercial viability. It follows that its strategies for achieving these objectives should form the central planks of its strategy rather than its supporting props.

One company which fully recognises this and acts accordingly is that which, for six years running, has been voted the USA's most admired company by a "jury" of over 8,000 senior executives, consultants and financial analysts. It ranked first on seven out of eight scales.

- The ability to attract, develop and keep talented people.
- Innovativeness.
- Financial soundness.
- Quality of products.
- Use of corporate assets.
- Value as a long-term investment.
- Environmental responsibility.

This corporation certainly qualifies as a talent-intensive company. It is Merck, one of the world's top pharmaceutical manufacturers. Asked to explain its success the company answer is that the key lies in its ability to attract, develop and keep good people. Richard Markham, head of worldwide marketing, said "We look at recruiting with the same kind of intensity as we do discovering new molecules in the lab." Merck's success is built on an extremely comprehensive strategy for the management of talent, described in the case study later on pages 187ff.

The slow adjustment of management thinking
Probably the most formidable obstacle standing in the way of a strategic approach to the management of talent is the difficulty most top executives have in grasping the full implications of the idea to which they pay lip-service: that in the talent-intensive organisation people are, indeed, the key assets and that talent is the only available source of enduring competitive advantage.

Why should this be so? It is partly due to the influence of traditional management thinking. The ideas underlying the practice of management were developed in the context of a set of industries which were labour-intensive rather than talent-intensive. In manufacturing small numbers of technologists – often self-taught – were required, but the major managerial task involved organising a labour force consisting of large numbers – often many thousands – of blue-collar workers, the majority of whom were unskilled or semi-skilled. In the service industries such as insurance or retailing it was a matter of directing armies of white-collar clerks and salespersons, literate and educated up to a point, but nevertheless performing relatively routine and undemanding work.

As discussed in Chapter 6, traditional tools and techniques for efficient manufacturing management, which began with Frederick Taylor, the inventor of scientific management, are inappropriate for the strategic management of talent. Taylor's approach rested on a number of assumptions. The first and most fundamental is that work is analysable into specific discrete actions and that it is programmable; that is, the desired output can be achieved by following a precisely predetermined sequence of steps. The second assumption is that, in general, managers are both more educated and more intelligent than the workforce and thus in a better position to decide how best jobs are to be done. The third assumption is that the exercise of discretion, initiative and spontaneity is detrimental to the efficient carrying out of work.

None of these assumptions is necessarily valid in any modern work situation, but clearly none has any validity in the case of high talent personnel and the kind of work we expect them to do. "Taylorism", nevertheless, is alive and well and is reflected in overambitious attempts to achieve very precise definitions of the nature of managerial work or to impose highly systematised control systems in R&D organisations.

The ideological framework for the management of the large "office" whether in commerce or as part of the machinery of government was laid down by the German sociologist, Max Weber. His *Theory of Social and Economic Organisation* was published in 1924, four years after his death. He remains the champion of bureaucracy, which he held to be the most efficient form of administration because it worked on an accepted basis of legitimate authority within a hierarchical structure, involving a framework of rationally thought-out rules and procedures designed to maximise authority. He saw the bureaucracy as a superior form of organisation compared with ones characterised by traditional (hereditary) authority or charismatic (personal) authority. He emphasised the value of the bureaucratic virtues: precision, speed, unambiguity, knowledge of files, continuity, discretion, unity, strict subordination, reduction of friction and of material and personal costs. He saw the positive aspects of a hierarchical structure, with each office subordinate to the one above it; every official's role determined by written rules; a regulated right of appeal; and the right to take grievances upwards.

Weber's system of organisation is no doubt well suited to an enterprise or agency with a task to perform which can be broken down into a number of routine sub-tasks, capable of standardisation with respect to both output and method and employing, relative to its overall size, a substantial proportion of unskilled or semi-skilled workers. It is a system of organisation appealing to those who place a high value on order, stability and security and to those who prefer to operate within a clear set of procedures and rules. The viability of such a system may be less questionable during periods of stable environmental conditions (if such ever exist) but it is ill-suited to changing conditions. Critics of bureaucracy would add that it stifles talent, particularly creativity, that its strong emphasis on seniority and hierarchy means that new ideas find great difficulty of expression and that mediocrity and avoidance of risk are more likely to be valued than exceptional talent.

The word "bureaucracy" is more closely associated with public service than with private-sector organisations, yet there is no doubt that large private-sector industrial organisations – such as General Motors or GE in the USA, ICI in the UK or the Anglo-Dutch oil company Shell – developed strong bureaucratic characteristics over many years which they have been shedding only relatively recently in the face of the need to change strategic direction rapidly and become more innovative. Nor can it be doubted that the bureaucratic ideal is present in the minds of many people at or near the top of large financial services organisations which have their roots in the organisational traditions of a past, more stable, era.

The confluence of these two streams of thought, subsequently developed by other thinkers and writers such as Henry Fayol, Lyndall F. Urwick, Alfred P. Sloan and Frank Gilbreth,[2] resulted in an approach to management based on analysis and measurement as the basis for decision-making and a set of beliefs about the design of effective organisations which emphasised such features as the chain of command, narrow spans of control, clear accountability and functional specialisation, all contributing to what Tom Peters has described as the "overlayered, underled" modern business corporation.

A second major influence on top management thinking has been the widespread acceptance of an analytical and rational approach to business strategy exemplified by the work of Michael Porter,[3] an economist by training, which is best described as "business strategy as if people did not matter". Porter argues that there are three basic ways to compete effectively in any market:

- to become the lowest-cost producer;
- to be the "differentiated" producer able to command a premium price as a consequence of the perceived additional value associated with the product or service; or
- to be the occupier of a specialist niche.

The weakness of this approach lies in the fact that none of these positions, once attained, can be sustained as a competitive advantage for very long. The low-cost producer will be challenged by companies with even better cost-control systems and even greater productivity gains. The "differentiated" producer will be challenged by "me too" competitors or by "leapfrogging" competitors coming out with products or services characterised by even greater added value. The occupier of a niche is the more likely to be eased out of it the more comfortable and profitable it is.

For talent-intensive companies there is no future in trying to be the lowest-cost producer. The whole purpose of attracting talented people is to add value by differentiation, not reduce cost. Both the other two market positions are tenable for a time but the ability of any enterprise to build a sustainable competitive advantage and defend its chosen positioning will be a function of its ability to stay ahead of the competition in terms of such things as product development, product innovation, quality of product or service and level of customer service. The ability of a company to do these things will rest in turn upon its ability to attract, retain, develop and motivate the best available talent.

Porter argues in his "value chain" analysis that there are five generic categories of "primary" activities involved in competing in any industry.

- Inbound logistics; that is, activities associated with receiving, storing and distributing inputs.
- Operations.
- Outbound logistics; that is, storing and distributing the final product or products.

- Marketing and sales.
- Service.

In a volume of over 500 pages only one is devoted to human-resource management, which is included under the heading of "support" activities along with procurement, technology development and "firm infrastructure", a loose bundle of activities ranging from general management to government relations and the legal department. For Porter, managing the parts warehouse is a primary function as far as competitiveness is concerned, whereas human-resource management is merely supportive. Yet in the only two paragraphs devoted to human resources he acknowledges that in some industries (unspecified) human-resource management holds the key to competitive advantage. He then quotes as an example a talent-intensive organisation, Arthur Andersen, which in his view draws a significant competitive advantage from its approach to recruiting and training its tens of thousands of professional staff.

Human-resource management holds the key to competitive advantage, not just in Arthur Andersen but in all talent-intensive organisations. The final case study for this book is of Merck, a benchmark for the strategic management of talent.

CASE STUDY

Merck

Merck's emergence as the USA's most admired company reflects an all-round set of achievements over a period of some years. Its growth and profitability have been outstanding. These achievements in turn have reflected its success not only in discovering new drugs but also in bringing them successfully to market.

It is a company in which the scientific and professional sub-culture is clearly the dominant one. The chief executive, Dr Roy Vagelos, was an NIH research scientist and university professor until the age of 45. He spent nine years as president of the Merck research laboratories before becoming corporate president. Although the company evidently has outstandingly competent managers and first-class marketing, the research laboratories remain its chief power base. The culture is a nice mixture of the "achievement" and "support" cultures. Achievement is defined as much in terms of contribution to "the continuing fight against suffering" as in contributing to the bottom line.

The company's philosophy stems from George W. Merck, son of the founder and himself a Harvard chemistry graduate, who established the laboratories in 1933. He expressed the company's credo in the following much-quoted phrase: "Medicine is for the patients. It is not for the profits. The profits follow, and if we have remembered that, they have never failed to appear. The better we have remembered that, the larger they have been."

The headquarters site at Rahway, New Jersey, where about a quarter of Merck's 19,000 US employees work, has much of the atmosphere of a university campus, especially in the research laboratories. Merck ploughs 11% of its sales back into research each year. Of the almost 3,000 people who work in the laboratories nearly a quarter have PhDs or other higher degrees.

The company's pay and benefits package is among the best in the USA. It seeks to compete in terms of salaries with the best in the country, not just in its field. There is a flexible benefits programme for salaried employees providing a wide range of choices, as well as a pension scheme and long-term disability insurance. There is also a save-as-you-earn scheme under which employees can save up to 15% of their salary and for every $2 the employee saves the company contributes $1 up to the first 5%.

There are strong education and training programmes and a highly sophisticated human-resources function which among other things constantly monitors the impact of Merck's policies on staff by means of regular opinion surveys. Results are compared with those of other leading companies belonging to a consortium known as the Mayflower Group which exists for the purpose of exchanging such information.

Another distinctive feature of Merck is a strong emphasis on "affirmative action": employing and providing equal opportunity for women and ethnic minorities.

Line management is very much involved in human-resources issues and activities. "I would say fully 98% of our actual recruiting is done by line management and usually line management at a significant level."

Unusually for a US firm which clearly has a strong set of values and beliefs, Merck has never extensively publicised them. About five years before the present study an outside consultant was commissioned to investigate Merck values with the aim of finding out the extent to which shared values existed despite never having been stated. The consultant found in interviews that the same 4–5 things kept coming up. One of the recommendations was that the company should not emblazon these over everything, but leave them implicit.

The company has a two-career track providing opportunities for scientific excellence as well as managerial competence. There is a process for identifying those with high potential, including a performance appraisal system designed to identify the top 5% performers, in the context of a wealth of talent. About 15% of a manager's performance rating is determined by "people-management objectives".

There are special motivational programmes for scientific personnel, the most significant of which is the Directors' Scientific Award which brings with it, as well as a monetary award, substantial public recognition and the opportunity to designate a school or institution to which the company will then make a sizeable contribution on the individual's behalf.

There is also, as previously described, a stock-option scheme for innovation which is "event-driven" in that the options are spread out over the various stages from basic research breakthrough, with the whole of an option being exercisable when, and only when, the innovation becomes successful in the marketplace.

There is an ongoing programme of organisation development which currently involves reducing the number of levels in the hierarchy and moving people much more than in the past across functions to improve their development, to increase mutual understanding between functions and to facilitate communications in order "to make the business seamless". Merck makes a great deal of use of multi-divisional and multi-functional taskforces which are seen as having a developmental function as well as achieving the particular objectives for which they were set up. There is a strong drive to institutionalise change in the organisation, to get people to accept that no matter how dazzling past successes have been there is a constant requirement to go on learning and to find out how to do things differently. Part of this approach is to encourage risk-taking.

Finally there is a worldwide management development programme delivered by such institutions as Columbia University in New York City, USA, Templeton College in Oxford and INSEAD in France.

The elements of a strategy for the strategic management of talent

Given that top management accepts the idea that talented people are the principal assets of the business and that the way they are managed does, indeed, provide the key to sustainable competitive advantage, we can now summarise the main elements of a strategic approach to getting the best out of talent.

1 Provide a clear sense of direction and purpose

The starting point for the strategic management of talent is the requirement to give talented people a common sense of purpose or direction and a set of shared beliefs and values. This is best done by involving the people concerned in the development of what Andrew Campbell[4] calls a "sense of mission". He points out that managers want more from their organisations than pay, security and the opportunity to develop their skills; they want a cause that is personally satisfying. This is equally true, if not more so, in respect of professional, technical and scientific personnel. Campbell makes an important distinction between the process of creating a sense of mission on the one hand and the process of writing a mission statement on the other. The latter is often little more than a public relations exercise whereas creating a sense of mission involves building consensus about strategy and developing a culture which is consistent with that strategy and supportive of actions to bring it about.

Among the companies in the present research the following stand out as having successfully created a strong sense of mission.

- Merck with its emphasis on "medicine is for the patients, not for the profits".
- Hewlett Packard and ICL with their clear statements of corporate goals and values: *The HP Way* and *The ICL Way*.
- Rockwell with its formal statement of mission.
- British Airways with its well-known mission to become the world's favourite airline.

In general, however, company statements of objectives were narrower than this, focusing mainly on objectives of a commercial nature expressed in a way unlikely to stir emotions or create a powerful sense of worth.

2 Develop an appropriate organisational framework

This means that the organisational context must be constantly reviewed in terms of its attractiveness as a setting for the work of talented people and in terms of its fit with the strategy.

In particular it is important to check out the following.

- Is the level of control such that on the one hand creative talent is not stifled and exceptionally able people have the autonomy and "space" that they need, yet on the other hand management has the information it needs to be able to judge the extent to which resources are being used productively?
- Given that the organisation needs different kinds of talent – in particular specialists in the field of its core business, highly competent managers and top-class sales personnel – how effective are the structural, procedural and cultural aspects of the organisation in integrating these three groups with their differing orientations and differing values systems into a cohesive organisation with shared beliefs and shared objectives? How effective are processes for integrating clerical and secretarial staff, maintenance technicians and production workers so that all feel part of the same business?
- Does the organisation have effective interfaces with relevant institutions in its environment: its universities, colleges, business schools, the scientific, technical and professional community, and so on? Does its reputation stand high in the eyes of the kinds of talented people it needs to attract?
- To what extent does the design of jobs and of work groups, the presence or absence of rules and procedures or the nature of the organisation's culture provide a setting which positively motivates talented people?
- Is the organisation sufficiently risk-taking and flexible so as to encourage needed levels of creativity and innovation and capacity to absorb change?

Virtually all the large organisations in the study were taking steps, or had recently done so, to reduce the number of levels in the hierarchy and most of the science-based companies were achieving integration of business and specialist functions through some form of matrix organisation.

It is clear, however, that in terms of creating an appropriate organisational setting for talented persons companies are laying much more emphasis on cultural factors than on structure or on systems and procedures. In some cases, notably IBM and Hewlett Packard, strong and clearly delineated corporate cultures were created by the organisations' founders. In other cases, too, a distinctive corporate culture has characterised the organisation over many years, due to the influence of a founder such as George Merck or a family as in the case of Solvay, even though the culture may not have been formalised or committed to paper. In some cases, however, the corporate culture is of relatively recent origin and reflects a form of social engineering or organisational architecture, designed to enlist people's commitment and focus their energies on corporate goals. Among the companies under review British Airways, ICL and GSI are outstanding examples of this kind.

3 Identification of future requirements for talent

The organisation's future needs for talent must be identified as rigorously as possible, both in quantitative and qualitative terms.

Again, virtually all the large businesses in the sample were concerned to identify their future requirements for high-talent personnel. Relatively few, however, having identified their longer-term needs, were maintaining their graduate recruitment at a level such that these needs would be met. Short-term considerations arising from the recessionary business conditions of 1991–92 meant that most companies were pursuing a financially driven approach to the issue rather than sticking to a strategic one.

4 Recruitment and selection

A pool of talent to meet this requirement must be recruited. The importance of this aspect of strategy will be acknowledged if top management is involved in the process and recruitment is not suspended because of a short-term business downturn. (Several respondents referred to the intensity amounting to obsessiveness with which they pursued the objective of attracting the most talented recruits.) The selection procedures used should be carefully chosen on the basis of evidence as to their relevance, reliability and validity. In the search for talent all avenues should be explored: within the business at all levels; in the community without discrimination on grounds of sex, race or religion; and on a global basis. Strong positive programmes of affirmative action in this respect are needed to overcome long-established traditional attitudes.

Despite the high reputation and visibility of the companies in the sample, reflected in huge numbers of unsolicited applications, there were few signs of complacency. Indeed the very companies most sought after by graduates seeking employment – Merck and British Airways, for example – were often the ones putting most effort into recruiting, treating it as a marketing exercise and involving line management at a senior level.

What was surprising, however, was the relative lack of sophistication in the selection methods in use. National Westminster Bank stands out in its use of full-scale assessment centre procedures at the recruiting stage. Few, other than British Airways, make very much use of psychometric tests although several companies reported having used them in the past. The main selection procedure in use remains the interview, or rather a series of interviews involving both human-resources specialists and line managers. One reason for a strong preference for this method is without doubt the fact that in many cases a vitally important selection criterion at this level of recruiting is whether or not the individual will fit in with the corporate culture.

More organisations are now casting their nets wide in the search for talent, increasing the range of educational institutions from which they are prepared to recruit, encouraging applications from women and ethnic minorities and engaging in international recruiting.

5 Identification of high potential

From within this pool of talent, once people have had the opportunity to demonstrate competence, the process of identifying those with exceptional talent and high potential must be carefully planned, giving particular attention to those in the core specialisms likely to develop into "hybrids" and become successful integrators once in managerial or marketing posts.

A recent survey of human-resources practices and priorities carried out by the consultants Towers Perrin showed that from the viewpoint of chief executives and senior line managers the most important task for the human-resources function today and also in the year 2000 is the identification of those with high potential. This is borne out by the very considerable efforts put into this activity by virtually all the companies of any size in the current study.

It was noticeable, however, that companies varied greatly in the extent to which these efforts embraced the professional, scientific and technical talent of the organisation or were concentrated on those selected *ab initio* for their general management potential. In the UK companies there was a tendency to neglect the specialists as a source of really high potential in the sense of tomorrow's top management. This was less marked in the USA, and UK practice was in marked contrast to that of most continental companies where it was assumed that the very top people of the future would be drawn from the ranks of the young engineers, chemists and other professionals of today.

No company was making systematic attempts to validate its assessment procedures.

6 Retention

There is a need for a clear strategy for ensuring that the top talent is retained. The building of emotional ties of loyalty, pride and commitment is likely to prove more effective in the long run than approaches based on financial incentives.

In the context of the economic recession the retention of staff was not a burning issue. Nevertheless, companies were conscious of the need to have policies to ensure retention of their most talented people and it was generally recognised that as well as building ties of loyalty the key factors were more to do with challenging work assignments and career development than with remuneration packages.

7 Managing for performance

Talented people must know what is expected of them in terms of outputs and be involved in setting their own performance standards. The achievement of these standards must be monitored through appraisal procedures which are suited to the kinds of people whose performance is under review, including peer appraisals. Support through counselling, coaching, mentoring and feedback mechanisms will assist people in the process of improving their performance.

Organisations differed widely in terms of how recently sophisticated performance appraisal systems had been developed and become accepted. In some instances such as IBM such a procedure has been a feature of company life for several decades. In other cases the human-resources function was still engaged in the delicate process of persuading highly talented and qualified staff to submit themselves to the process. Nowhere was any complacency found; the search for a better performance appraisal system is clearly never ending.

8 Motivating

Rewards and forms of recognition must be flexible, so that groups of people with different needs, values and motives can all find opportunities for achieving their personal goals.

Given that most highly talented people are strongly motivated by the work itself and by their need to put their talents to use there is a danger, reflected in the attitude of some companies, of taking their motivation for granted. In the UK this tendency was reinforced by a reluctance, stemming from the UK culture, to use special award schemes or other highly visible forms of recognition along the lines of Rockwell's Leonardo da Vinci Medallion or the Directors' Scientific Award scheme of Merck. With considerable justification some of the smaller companies such as GSI, SAS Institute and Coley Porter Bell saw the culture and spirit of the organisation as the principal motivating force.

9 Developing

A range of opportunities is needed for the further development of talent, from formal education and training programmes through to planned work experience. In particular, this must focus on providing challenging work assignments and accept that the lessons of experience are gained from failures as well as successes.

Most of the large companies were relying chiefly on a "ladder" or series of in-company management development programmes related to various career stages or milestones. The use of external courses at business schools was mainly confined to the most senior levels. The company programmes were concerned more with imparting company philosophies, strategies and practices than with the development of the individual. Indeed, development of individuals was seen as more likely to come out of challenging work experiences than from attending courses.

10 Evaluation

The impact of the company's human-resource strategies must be continuously evaluated, in terms of both cost-benefit analysis, wherever this is possible, and of their impact on employee attitudes and satisfactions. IBM has pioneered the way for many years in conducting employee opinion surveys at regular intervals. For an organisation of any size, employing large numbers of talented people, the opinion survey is an indispensable strategic tool.

It nevertheless remains the case that in the last analysis the test of a human-resources strategy lies in the achievements of the people concerned and in the reflection of those achievements in the business results. In specific industries the achievements of the talented specialists are to be found in a variety of ways: patents awarded, new products launched, prize-winning designs, the spotting of a new pop-music star, the successful negotiating of major financial deals, and so on. Such individually based triumphs do not of themselves, however, guarantee business success and it is in the quality of management that the final, key ingredient is to be found. The organisations in the current study are all, in their respective fields, successful – some of them outstandingly so – and this success reflects the balance they have achieved between specialist know-how and general management competence.

The danger that comes with success, however, is complacency and without doubt the biggest difference found between the companies in the study – irrespective of size, industry, nationality or degree of success achieved – was the extent to which they were still learning, self-critical and open to new ideas on the one hand, or complacent, knowing all the answers and self-satisfied on the other. The attitude of some of the companies approached to take part in the study was that they saw the issues involved in the management of talent as vitally important, they felt they had more to learn than to teach others, but they very much wanted to share what they had learned so far. Others expressed little interest in what other companies might be doing but were pleased to describe their own practices which they clearly believed could scarcely be improved upon.

The last word: the key role of the chief executive

In the talent-intensive organisation the key task of the chief executive is to articulate the connection between the economic aims of the enterprise, represented by such objectives as growth in earnings per share or increased competitiveness, and the desire of talented people to experience in their work the fulfilment of their needs to be creative, to solve problems, to work at the leading edge of science or technology; in other words to excel in their chosen profession or vocation.

In many cases among the companies studied the chief executive came from the ranks of those whose talents are linked to the core technology of the business. Such individuals can bridge gaps in values and create cultures in which both managers and specialists are heroic figures. The chief executives who lack such a background have to work harder to achieve these things.

This issue makes clear the distinction between management and leadership. An individual appointed to run a talent-intensive organisation on the strength of his or her track record as a manager will need, in order to enthuse talented professional and scientific personnel with challenging commercial goals, outstanding qualities of leadership as well.

In particular he or she will need to pay attention to the following.

- Getting to know the top talent in the organisation and building strong personal relationships.
- Being willing to change attitudes, adjust mindsets and see things from others' viewpoints.

- Perhaps most important of all, learning how to get just as excited by a new breakthrough in knowledge or a new product idea as by improvements in the bottom line.

It was not possible to meet many chief executives during the course of this study; most of the requests for information were referred to the human-resources function. In the UK those that did give personal interviews – Keith Bedell-Pearce of Prudential Financial Services; Jan Hall of Coley Porter Bell; John Ockenden, chairman of Data Logic; Ken Parker of CMG – all clearly met the above criteria. It is clear too, from information which is widely available, that the same is true of many others, with outstanding UK examples in Sir Colin Marshall of British Airways and Peter Bonfield of ICL. In the USA Roy Vagelos of Merck provides an equally clear role model. It is to such people that others of outstanding ability turn for leadership and guidance. Theirs is the talent for leadership, which is perhaps the rarest talent of them all.

References
1 Amin Rajan, *Capital People*, London, London Human Resources Group, 1991.
2 For a summary of the ideas of these writers see Carol Kennedy, *Guide to the Management Gurus*, London, Business Books, 1991.
3 Michael Porter, *Competitive Advantage*, New York, The Free Press, 1985.
4 Andrew Campbell, Marion Devine and David Young, *A Sense of Mission*, London, Hutchinson Business Books, 1990

APPENDIX

PARTICIPATING COMPANIES AND
THEIR PERSONNEL

Computers and electronics

Data General (USA)
Robert F. Vitale, Corporate Director, Human Resources

Hewlett Packard (USA)
Neil M. Johnston, Director of Corporate Education

Hewlett Packard Laboratories (UK)
Gwenda Ward, Personnel Manager

IBM (UK)
Sir Leonard Peach, Personnel Director

ICL (UK)
Don Beattie, Personnel Director
Andrew Mayo, Personnel Director, ICL Europe

Intel Corporation (USA)
Carlene M. Ellis, Vice-President, Director of Human Resources
Yvonne Lenbergs, Staffing Manager

Motorola Corporation (USA)
Pat Canavan, Vice-President and Corporate Director, Human
Resources

Philips International BV (Netherlands)
John D. de Leeuw, Managing Director, Corporate Staff Bureau

Thomson SA (France)
Mme Martin Bridegain, Group Director, Human Resources

Software engineering and consulting

AT&T Istel (UK)
Chris Haynes, Director of Advanced Technology

CMG Computer Management Group (UK)
Ken Parker, Chief Executive

Data Logic (UK)
John Ockenden, Chairman

GSI (France)
Jean Francis Cottin, Director

SAS Institute (USA)
David Russo, Director of Human Resources
Betty Fried, Manager, Corporate Communications

Other high-technology companies

ABB (Switzerland)
Arne Olsson, Corporate Staff Management Resources

British Aerospace (UK), Military Aircraft Division
Judith Tolland, Head of Human Resource Development

Eastman-Kodak Company (USA)
George E. Davies, Director, Executive Resources and Human
Resource Strategy

European Space Agency (France)
Réné Oosterlink, Head of Personnel and Site Development

GEC-ALSTHOM (France)
Guy Schmitt, Director, Management Development and Training

GE-CGR (France)
Jean Yves Lagière, Manager, Professional Relations, Human
Resource Division

Rockwell International (USA)
Thomas D. Sumrall, Vice-President, Management Planning
Allen G. Bormann, Corporate Director, College Relations and
Recruiting

Thorn-EMI Central Research Laboratories (UK)
Don Brunton, Director of Administration and Finance

United Technologies Corporation (USA)
Regina M. Hitchery, Director, Leadership Development

Xerox Corporation (USA)
Joseph F. Charlton, Vice-President, Corporate Research and
Technology

Chemicals, pharmaceuticals and healthcare

Baxter International Inc. (USA)
Anthony J. Rucci, Senior Vice-President Human Resources, Vice-
President Human Resource Planning and Staffing
Maria T. Rubley, Vice-President, Baxter Management Institute

Bayer AG (Germany)
Professor Kleine-Weishede, Director, Human Resources

Colgate Palmolive Company (USA)
R. Alicia Whitaker, Director, Global Staffing, Career Planning
and Learning

Glaxo Group Research Ltd (UK)
John Hume, Director of Human Resources

L'Oréal (France)
François Vachery, Vice-President, Director General of Human
Resources

Merck & Co. Inc. (USA)
Arthur Stromer, Executive Director Human Resources, Strategies
and Policies
James E. Higgins, Executive Director, Manpower Management

Smith & Nephew, Europe, Ltd (UK)
R.M. Cater, European Human Resources Director

Solvay SA (Belgium)
Roland Simon and Daniel de Bouvere

Financial services

Harlow Butler Ueda (UK) (money brokers)
Jacqui Lewis, Director of Personnel

Kleinwort Benson (UK)
Chris Palmer, Group Personnel Director

Marsh, McLennan and Companies Inc. (USA)
Fran N. Bonsignore, Senior Vice-President, Human Resources
and Administration
A.J.C. Smith, Chief Operating Officer
Barbara Perlmutter, Vice-President Corporate Communications

J.P. Morgan (USA)
Herbert J. Hefke, Senior Vice-President Human Resources
Anthony E. Beale, Managing Director, Morgan Guarantee Trust
Co.

National Westminster Bank (UK)
David Strowger, Assistant General Manager, Personnel

Prudential Corporation (UK)
Keith Bedell-Pearce, Chief Executive, Prudential Financial
Services Ltd
Geoffrey Keeys, Group Personnel Director

Willis Coroon (UK)
David Podd, Personnel Director, Willis Coroon Group Services Ltd

Rudolf Wolff (UK) (financial futures brokers)
P.L. Holland

Miscellaneous

Anspach, Grossman, Portugal Inc. (USA)
Joel B. Portugal, Partner

British Broadcasting Corporation (UK)
Bob Nelson, Head of Corporate Management Development

British Airways (UK)
Eva Lauermann, General Manager, Human Resources
Coley, Porter, Bell (UK)
Jan Hall, Chairman, Kareen Hood and Bill Walmsgrove
(Directors)

Continental AG (Germany)
Wolfdieter Gogoll, Education and Training Department

Egon Zehnder (UK)
Robin Gowlland

EMI Music International (UK)
Patrick Spenser, Personnel Director

Longman Group (UK)
Angela Mansell, Director, Human Resources (publishing)

Sotheby's (UK)
Chris Mead, Personnel Director

INDEX